IDEOLOGY

IDEOLOGY

Structuring Identities in Contemporary Life

GORDON BAILEY
and
NOGA GAYLE

Originally published by Broadview Press 2003

National Library of Canada Cataloguing in Publication

Bailey, Gordon, 1946–
    Ideology : structuring identities in contemporary life / Gordon Bailey and Noga Gayle.

Includes bibliographical references and index.
ISBN 1-44260-085-0
(PREVIOUS ISBN 1-55111-506-9)

1. Ideology. 2. Socialization. I. Gayle, Noga II. Title.

HM641.B33 2003   303.3'72   C2003-901928-4

We welcome comments and suggestions regarding any aspect of our publications–please feel free to contact us at the addresses below or at news@utphighereducation.com

North America
5201 Dufferin Street, North York, Ontario, Canada, M3H5T8
Tel: (416) 978-2239 ; Fax: (416) 978-4738
email: customerservice@utphighereducation.com
2250 MILITARY ROAD, TONAWANDA, NY, USA 14150

UK, Ireland, and continental Europe
Plymbridge Distributors Ltd.
Estover Road,
Plymouth, PL6 7PY, UK
Tel: (01752) 202301; Fax: (01752) 202333
email: orders@plymbridge.com

Higher Education University of Toronto Press gratefully acknowledges the financial support of the Government of Canada through the Book Publishing Industry Development Program for our publishing activities.

This book is printed on acid-free paper containing 30% post-consumer fibre.

Eco-Logo Certified
30 % Post.

PRINTED IN CANADA

Contents

Acknowledgments

We would like to thank a number of people for their commitment and conscientious efforts to bring this book to completion. At a crucial moment in its development, William K. Carroll provided us with a critical review that gave us new energy and perspective. Our special thanks to Betsy Struthers for her sensitive, meticulous editorial work. Her comments throughout this process were perceptive and much appreciated.

In the early stages, Donald A. Bailey gave the manuscript a thorough reading and indicated useful directions that subsequently were reiterated by others. Eventually, we got to most of them.

Michael Harrison of Broadview Press has given us a good deal of support and insight into pathways that could make the book the best possible.

We thank Hazel Henderson for permission to use her diagram, "Total Productivity System of an Industrial Society," from *Paradigms in Progress,* copyright © 1982, Hazel Henderson (San Francisco, CA: Berrett-Koehler Publishers, 1995).

We would also like to thank our partners, Sue Bailey and Bill Ignatiuk, for their tireless efforts, editing and otherwise, to bring this book to publication.

Finally, we thank our students in various courses at Capilano College who have worked with some of the early versions of this text, responding with both criticism and encouragement.

We dedicate the book to our families.

CHAPTER 1

The Overt and Covert Power of Ideology

> Several years before, Mother had fought Father, first about the fabric that the veil was made of and then about the *haik*, or traditional long cloak that women wore in public.
>
> The traditional veil was a rectangular piece of white cotton so heavy that it made the simple act of breathing a real accomplishment. Mother wanted to replace it with a tiny triangular black veil made of sheer silk chiffon. This drove Father crazy: "It is so transparent! You might as well go unveiled!" But soon the small veil, the *litham*, became the fashion, with all the nationalists' wives wearing it all over Fez....
>
> The *haik* was made of seven long meters of heavy white cotton cloth that you had to drape around yourself. You then had to hold on to the ends of the *haik*, awkwardly tied up under your chin, to keep it from falling off.... The *djellaba*, on the other hand, was a closely fitted man's robe with a hood, slits in the sides to allow long strides, and trimmed sleeves which left your hands completely free.... So the daughters started wearing the men's *djellaba*, and soon thereafter, their mothers followed suit. To discourage Mother from joining in, Father commented regularly on the revolution that he was witnessing in the Medina streets. "It is like the French women trading their skirts for men's pants," he said. "And if women dress like men, it is more than chaos, it is *fana* (the end of the world)." (Mernissi, 1994: 118).

The elements that shape a person's thinking about or acting on any particular experience are always, in part, a mystery. Everyday we make decisions about what to wear, what to do, and what forms of entertainment interest us; we make choices about friends and family and how to respond to them. Some of these decisions seem conscious and deliberate, others seem to be made below the level of conscious decision-making. Some involve us directly, others seem guided by social, political, or economic forces or by corporate profit motives well outside our immediate experience. The branding of our clothing and other articles of everyday life now seems taken for granted.

These everyday choices or decisions are guided partially by our socio-cultural environment and partially by our conditioned responses. But by whom or what are they conditioned?

One of social science's great tensions is whether we make individually driven or societally driven decisions. Our society tells us that we are individuals who are free to choose everything from laundry detergent to beer, these choices supposedly guided by a media-sanctified individual intelligence or individualistic ethic. However, when we pause to reflect we "know" that these choices are often dictated by fad or fashion, that we are caught in a T-shirt or baseball cap form of dialogue with others in our communities.

Ideologies, at the simplest level, are systems of beliefs that guide our choices and behaviours and, indeed, justify our thoughts and actions. It's intriguing to imagine how much thought went into a person's choice of a T-shirt that expresses the following: "Once you've hugged a person, you'll never go back to trees." Such messages are ideologically loaded – they defend or attempt to establish different or new political terrain. But other examples might seem less preconsidered. For example, a Charlie Brown (Peanuts) T-shirt may simply show a person's love of the cartoon character and his or her perspective on life. At another level of analysis, such a T-shirt might express that the person is far too locked into media presentation and **representation** of the "good life." We make judgments, which, if inspected, typify our ideological orientation or perspective.

The experiences related by Fatima Mernissi—her memories of her life from an argument at home between her mother and father to the busy streets she walked along, the clothes worn by the women and girls, and the tensions of the culture all around her—are laden with questions of power.

The contradictions of her father's and mother's needs, the gendered nature of her perspective, the dire warnings of the dangers of change, and the breaking down of seemingly fixed patterns: all of these relate to questions of value, to what matters, and to questions of power. Contested moments in life—like the intense disagreement between her mother and father over apparel—may seem to be culturally determined, but moments like these occur in every culture. At times they are like lightning bolts as they hit, crack open, or shatter ideas and practices that once seemed to be fully protected. At other times the forces embedded in our everyday experiences are difficult to see, and then, even if we recognize them, they can be just as difficult to face. Sometimes our perceptions can be shrouded by fear, but more often the sheer ordinariness of experience masks the power of the belief systems that shape our worlds. They are too much within our lives. They are so close that we are unable to see them.

Many of us—at least those of us who are parents—could say how much we have learned from our daughters or sons, whether as mothers or fathers. But much of what we've learned is often deeply embedded, hidden below our level of awareness. We may be able to recognize the changing times, the "new." It is one thing to acknowledge the learning we have done—the sharing of our daughter's understanding of clothing, her sense of fashion, or her expression of control over her appearance; it is another to ascribe power to the modern, the changing, the innovative, the simple expressive convention or convenience of dress—to recognize that this dynamic of change is driven by the closely felt needs of a historical period that we call modern times. The idea within this particular frame or enclosure—"thereafter, the mothers followed suit"—joins together the experiential and the ideological.

On an individual basis, every day each one of us has to determine what is important at a particular moment or even in general. Life doesn't always, or even often, shake itself out into nice little batches of either this or that. Time after time we have to choose an action or an idea, often with little tangible information, experience, or knowledge. Sometimes we figure things out consciously, but more often we seem to make our choices almost automatically, or subconsciously.

What is it that guides our tentative, if not at times totally tenuous, actions and thoughts? In the first place, we have to learn how to recognize the existence of these actions and thoughts, how to find their roots and pull them out. We need to learn how to recognize the beliefs, feelings, desires, ideas, conceptual frameworks, guidance systems, methodologies, management systems—call them what you will—that form our actions and ideas in everyday life. Otherwise we would be suggesting that the guidance systems of human life are not systems at all, but are beyond understanding. We would be in part accepting an inability to make daily choices and make sense of our lives. We could slip into **narcosis**— into sleep or a stupor that clouds our view of the world.

Whether we want to admit it or not, we really do construct our lives in ways that are contained by categories of thought. Friedrich Nietzsche (1844–1900) called this run of daily experience "*making* equal what is new," or fitting the unknown (things that are happening to us in the immediate present) into the known (our past experience). "In *our* thought," he said, "the essential feature is fitting new material into old schemas [sic], *making equal what is new*" (Nietzsche, 1967: 273). What might seem haphazard is more often an active rather than a passive process of determination, however deeply hidden.

These hidden (and sometimes not so hidden), often less than conscious categories of thought, these belief systems, are the substance of **ideology**— the very complex concept that, as we will see, can have many meanings and is the subject of much debate. Indeed, of all the terms used in the social sciences to help clarify the nature of social reality—to clarify understandings of social structure, social experience, and social theory—ideology is perhaps one of the most difficult to pin down. For those encountering it for the first time, it is a particularly difficult term. Nonetheless, ideology is also one of the most often employed words in social analysis, whether in academia or the media. It is a term with tremendous conceptual power, yet it regularly precipitates conceptual confusion. The term's very ambiguity in some way indicates its strength and its power to control and manipulate debate. Often, rather than helping to explain the world, the conflicting perspectives engendered by the term reveal its conflicts and complexities. But what we know as "ideologies" can also falsify or simplify, masking these complexities. This is particularly evident, for instance, when we examine the place of fundamentalist, literalist, religious, and ideological formations or political approaches that break everything down into simplistic "us and them" solutions.

For our purposes here, we will begin with a dictionary definition (we will get to the more complex and changing meanings of the concept in Chapter 2). Ideology is "a system of ideas or way of thinking, usually relating to politics or society, or to the conduct of a class or group, and regarded as justifying actions, especially one that is held implicitly or adopted as a whole and maintained regardless of the course of events" (*The Canadian Oxford Dictionary*, 1998). Even that is not so simple.

Basically, to study ideologies, or a particular ideology, is to survey the determinants that create the conditions of our lives—conditions that in turn create our identities. Understanding these determinants, understanding ideology in all its shapes, can elevate what we share with others to the level of consciousness. To begin the study of ideology demands an understanding of how we, as a society, come to common agreements and how these common agreements have come to be part of us. How is it that we actually communicate?

For us, the explanation for these phenomena combines "socialization" (the process by which people learn to conform to social norms, becoming members of society) with ideology-building and ideology-maintaining. Socialization often makes us take something for granted; it can hide or bury "ideology." This explanation necessarily raises issues of power. By its very nature, although socialization to an ideological position or ideology is not a conspiratorial act on the part of adults, parents, the media, or the **state**, it is still an act of power, of advantage.

Power and Ideology

Since the attacks on the World Trade Center and the Pentagon on September 11, 2001, the use of the word "ideology"—as well as the concept itself—has gained a new, and to some extent different, currency. The atmosphere surrounding what has become known as the "aftermath" of that particular day (including the war that emerged from it), has become permeated with ideology, in the most contradictory ways. Politicians and journalists, as well as everyday people, generated ideological perspectives to identify personal position, global political position, and religious orientations or sentiment, and to define what debates can and cannot be aired. There seems to have been a distinct increase in ideological naming, at times name-calling. Often it seems that the other person is ideological, while the person doing the speaking is somehow closer to the so-called truth.

It is really no great wonder that ideology has once again come so strongly to the fore. It has long been one of the most important concepts in social analysis. In academic study, the concept fits within the framework of the **sociology of knowledge**, including both the production and **reproduction** of knowledge. It is a concept, we believe, that needs to be grounded within experience, and in the following text we make that connection by way of case studies, historical examples, and social observations. However, ideology, as it is experienced, is both generated and sustained. We undergo ideological perspectives, and we participate in their creation and maintenance. In our view, this connection is the central dynamic if critical understanding is to lead to social action constructed out of social analysis—in other words, to social **praxis**.

For example, in an exploration of the notions of race, class, and gender the underlying, taken-for-granted power relationships in contemporary society often deny the internal complexities of group realities, such as the diversity of women, ethnic differences, or economic disparities or barriers to success. In part, these power dynamics become a buffer to social understanding because of the point of reference, the place out of which these analyses arise. From the perspective of writer bell hooks, the **discourse** on race, for instance, sets up "White, Supremacist, Capitalist, Patriarchy" as the reference point (hooks, 1997). White women's realities become "universalized" in representation and social interactions. What we need to do, then, is disclose the mechanisms that allow for this dominance.

Another example might include the formations characterized as "fundamentalist Christianity" or "fundamentalist Islam," or we might look at who represents the various forms of religiosity within various societies. We might question the basic underlying ideological premises that triggered the president of the United States to declare, as he simplified the complex historical moment of the horrific attacks of September 11, 2001,

"Every nation, in every region, now has a decision to make. Either you are with us, or you are with the terrorists" (Bush, 2001). Or why he then suggested shopping, or consumerism, as a way for ordinary Americans to show that they were not devastated by the crisis and that life could go on as usual. Looking further abroad, we might also begin to weave the threads of social existence together and see that the lives of many of the women of Afghanistan have remained committed to both the material realities of their existence and the ideological realities that have so affected them. Their intent is to emerge from the ashes, recognizing the complexities of everyday life for themselves and their children. The nature and interconnectedness of religion, consumerism, and the oppression of women gain overall clarity if we can recognize their ideological underpinnings.

Our exploration of ideology recognizes the centrality that the structures and systems of power and advantage maintain in developing *points of view*; in other words, how they mediate people's understandings of society. It is as if we see the world through ideological lenses. We need to better understand the use of these lenses and consider how our language helps to form the conceptual/material origins of our thought and to shape how we interpret the public and private experiences and domains within which we live, locally and globally, within private and public spaces.

The excitement that further drives the study of ideology, therefore, is its relationship to power and the distribution of such power in society. In questioning this relationship, we have the opportunity to achieve both a new moment of understanding and a new moment for social action—action based on democratic human relations. Our objective here is to uncover the ideological forces, the theoretical moments, and the real conditions facing people today. We recognize that to confront the powerful, ideological dimensions of our lives we must be responsible to them and for them. We must participate as democratically entitled **citizens**. This is, in our view, an exciting and exploratory process.

In the words of Noam Chomsky, "My personal feeling is that citizens of the democratic societies should undertake a course of intellectual self-defense to protect themselves from manipulation and control, and to lay the basis for a meaningful democracy" (Chomsky, 1989: vii-viii). That, too, is our project here.

The Concept of Ideology

The concept of ideology has deep roots within our society. It is also a term that has little or no history in commonplace language and is usually used only in educational or academic work or sometimes in newspaper opinion pieces (though rarely in regular reporting). Yet, as we have seen, the concept did become especially prominent after September 11, 2001. President Bush described the events of that day as an all-out assault on the "American way of life" and a war on "freedom and **democracy**"— which are of course (ideological) concepts as opposed to facts (such as, for instance, that it was an attack on skyscraper towers containing corporate offices filled with not only white, Anglo-Saxon workers but also Puerto Rican, Sri Lankan, Indian, and many other ethnic minority Americans). As *The New Internationalist* put it: "Quickly the assault was turned into ideology—instead of an act carried out against the unsuspecting and the innocent, it became an 'Attack on America' in the phrase of CNN. The flesh-and-blood victims have been transformed by President Bush's words into faceless pawns in a simplistic struggle between good and evil" (November 2001: 4).

Clearly, ideology can carry people off to war. It can also have a profound impact upon our everyday lives in ways that usually go unnoticed. Social observers (for example, Althusser, 1969) continue to be amazed by how hidden and below the level of consciousness ideologies really are. Certainly, the more we understand its impact, the more alert we will be to our social circumstances and surroundings.

As we will see (Chapter 2), the definitions of "ideology" are many and varied and can change over time. Given this complexity, our work as social scientists, whether as beginning students of the discipline or seasoned veterans, is to recognize in some way what we and others are talking about when we speak of "ideology" and to call into question those aspects of our lives that are taken for granted or remain more or less hidden. As we investigate the meanings, understandings, and impact of ideologies upon our lives, we need to become alert to the genesis of their power within our own experience and their role at a more general level within the power structures of our society. This project involves maintaining a certain degree of engagement with events at both the individual and societal levels, as well as the level of the state. Following Cornel West's advice that "demystification is the most illuminating mode of theoretical inquiry" (West, 1993: 213), we need to reflect upon our own experience. The very act of reflection, though at times it may seem passive, can often lead to action or, possibly, to some kind of activist mentality.

Making sense of society is a demanding, exciting, and occasionally disheartening experience. Sometimes, the more sense one makes of society, the more distant seem social justice or significant social change. But then, such statements, in and of themselves, appear to have ideological qualities; we must keep alert to our own words and idea structures as we present them. Usually, our conceptual frameworks are so set or settled into our consciousness that we seldom work at gaining familiarity with them. They are the "eye through which we see" (see Chapter 4, p. 76) and we all know how much we take our eyes for granted. In addition, this particular domain of learning and understanding—the domain of ideology—has largely avoided disciplined and rigorous investigation at almost every level of institutionalized education, which has only served to leave room open for the imposition of structures of oppression. To be curious about and explore our conceptual frames are the first acts of a liberatory intelligence. This process is also perhaps the longest of life's journeys. The intricate architecture of the mind is built on an array of perceptions and conceptions that are difficult to recognize and in effect difficult, at times, to articulate.

Therefore, our project is to recognize the complexity of our own conceptualizations, to explore not only their origins but also the basic processes and content that shape and construct our emergent identities. We need to ask what frames or lenses we use to view the social world and to guide our actions within it. For example, how are we socialized and conditioned through our families, our schools, and our media-entertainment systems to understand the norms, values, and mores of our culture and society? As someone reflecting on the continuing struggles in Ireland commented, "Who are we conditioned to hate?" That is an important and basic question.

Frameworks for Social Analysis

Typically, in our attempts to make sense of both such questions and our social world, we adopt certain theoretical models or frameworks. Often these adopted frameworks remain below the level of our consciousness and are taken for granted, or, if they are brought out into the open they are not vigilantly studied. In essence, we need to recognize them and continuously and rigorously apply them to our everyday lives.

In sociology a number of theoretical models provide profound and timeless perspectives on these matters. Historically, sociology has explored social realities within several frameworks: **consensus theory**, exemplified by the work of Emile Durkheim; **conflict theory**, embodied in the work of Karl Marx and Max Weber; and the **micro-theory** explored by George Herbert Mead, Charles Horton Cooley, and Erving Goffman, among others. More recently, the feminist perspective and cultural studies theorists have joined in: theorists such as Dorothy Smith, Jessie Bernard, bell hooks, Patricia Hill-Collins, Himani Bannerji, Cornel West, Stuart Hall, and others have contributed a major new emphasis to social analysis.

In some ways, though, these categories themselves become ideological enclosures, historically laden with hardened, sedimented baggage, rather than being illuminating conceptualizations. Attempting to unravel the power and impact of the term "ideology" will often mean finding new ways of seeing things.

What follows is a somewhat eclectic approach to social analysis; it combines the work and perspectives of a number of different theories and theorists. It also demands that students of society not only recognize the intersection of the social inequalities of gender, race, and class, but also, in the work of theorizing, recognize the role of **identity politics**—what Madan Sarup refers to as "communities of interests" (Sarup, 1996: 52)—which not only asserts that groups have a multiplicity of **identity** formations, but also that they exert control over how these identities are portrayed or represented within the political complexities of modern or **postmodern** society.

We begin with the connection of experience and ideology, and the contradictions that surface from this standpoint. To establish these connections, we will look at the work of two theorists, who make their starting point the lived historical experience of people and societies. Both, in very different ways, unite the **macro-theory** (larger, overarching) picture of society with the **micro-theory** (smaller, detailed) immediate view of everyday life. For our purposes, one of them, C. Wright Mills, concentrates on the relationship between private troubles and public issues. The other, Karl Marx, emphasizes issues of historical **dialectical materialism**.

C. Wright Mills

Almost all sociological perspectives see the work of C. Wright Mills as being central to understanding the **contextualization** of social phenomena. Mills's recognition of the relationship between the microexperience of individuals and the macrorealities of social structure establishes the importance of what he calls **the sociological imagination.** Mills takes us through moments of experience that explore relationships between the personal troubles of certain milieu and the public issues of social structure:

> *Troubles* occur within the character of the individual and within the range of his immediate relations with others; they have to do with his self and with those limited areas of social life of which he is directly and personally aware.....*Issues* have to do with matters that transcend these local environments of the individual and the range of his inner life. ... An issue is a public matter: some value cherished by publics is felt to be threatened. Often there is a debate about what that value really is and about what it is that really threatens it. This debate is often without focus if only because it is the very nature of an issue, unlike even widespread trouble, that it cannot very well be defined in terms of the immediate and everyday environments of ordinary men. (Mills, 1959: 8–9)

From this conceptual beginning, Mills goes on to consider examples of social phenomena such as divorce and unemployment statistics within communities and societies—all as a means of illuminating the relationship and linkages between levels of experience and analysis. Establishing both the link between biography and history and recognizing the range of human experience and yet the continuities of human relationships provides a depth of understanding beyond the taken-for-granted level. In essence, this project stimulates an analysis that transcends the immediate, yet is activated by it and within it. This task is crucial to social analysis. In his work Mills succinctly cuts to the moment of conceptual significance:

> In so far as war is inherent in the **nation-state** system and in the uneven industrialization of the world, the ordinary individual in his restricted milieu will be powerless ... to solve the troubles this system or lack of system imposes upon him. In so far as the family as an institution turns women into darling little slaves and men into their chief providers and unweaned dependents, the problem of a satisfactory marriage remains incapable of purely private solution. In so far as the overdeveloped megalopolis and the overdeveloped automobile are built-in features of an overdeveloped society, the issues of urban living will not be solved by personal ingenuity and private wealth. (Mills, 1959: 10)

Now, as we encounter the twenty-first century, 40 years after Mills wrote this passage, the "overdeveloped automobile" still reigns. Although a few critics have attacked the power of the automobile to govern and control daily life, society as a whole has come to take it almost for granted and few of us can imagine "divorcing" our cars (see Alvord, 2000). Why is this so? How are we socialized to these ideologies and how do we learn over time to accept them at such a taken-for-granted level within our consciousness?

B. Singh Bolaria, in working through Mills's conceptualization of these considerations, counterpoints the dynamics of blame: "**defective individuals**" versus "**faulty structures**" (Bolaria, 1995: 3). For example, are the homeless people of our societies lazy, good-for-nothings or are they people who have been marginalized or structured out of a social system that advantages some and seriously disadvantages others? There is a tension embedded in human relationships — from the site of blame to the moment of struggle, from the site of **resistance** to the attempt to move beyond ideological interpretation to an analysis based on a view of social justice. How does Mills's understanding of social phenomena activate our daily reflections and the way in which we forge particular understandings within our communities and circles of relationships? Are our actions governed by the social structural issues that form the context of our lives? How are our biographies shaped by their historical setting? For example, has recognition of the existence of date rape changed the sexual behaviours of men and women within our society? Has it only significantly changed the behaviours of women, because they are alert to the injury and hurt that they might/can/possibly/will experience? Do we assume that experience or self-interest is our one, and only, teacher?

Ideology inhabits our everyday world at multiple levels. Our lives and identities are layered, and it is through these layers that we negotiate our existence. Reality at the individual level of social action does not always coincide with reality at the state level. For example, some people dismiss immigrants as not contributing to society and regard them as parasites. Yet, the state itself recognizes immigration as an important element in the building of a healthy, vibrant economy. Of particular importance are immigrants classified as "entrepreneurial," a category that requires entrants to employ a certain number of Canadians as a basic condition of their immigration. Those classified as independent immigrants are required to be within the ages of 15 to 45, a range that represents the most productive period of a person's life. Sponsors of those applying to immigrate in the family sponsorship class are required to demonstrate that their income is sufficient to prevent those sponsored from becoming wards of the state. We need to explore the presentation of knowledge surrounding this issue to comprehend the complexities of immigration from the macropicture to the daily lives of immigrants themselves and the daily lives of the population into which they are moving.

How, then, can individuals learn to appreciate the intricate connections regarding issues that affect their everyday lives? Keeping informed might be the answer—but anyone who turns a critical eye on media presentations might well be discouraged in this endeavour. Although we are constantly bombarded with media information—whether from television, radio, books, or magazines—the information received tends to be fragmented, with limited context, and based on limited sources. Often, issues are presented ahistorically or without extended connections. For example, news accounts do not analyze the dramatic global economic restructuring that is taking place simultaneously with the restructuring in immigration policy. There is little public discussion, for instance, on the impact of trade agreements or the increasing **hegemony** of multinational corporations on jobs and the realities of immigrant lives. To begin the process of becoming active participants within our society we need to recognize the ideological formations involved in these kinds of issues as well as the impact of ideology on our daily life decisions—which brings us to the significance and importance of Karl Marx's fundamental understanding of **dialectical materialism.**

Karl Marx

Despite rumours to the contrary, Karl Marx's place in contemporary social thought and, indeed, social/economic/political life, is anything but dead. Indeed, some contemporary thinkers—for example, John Ralston Saul (1994)—have remarked that the real custodians of Marxism are the CEOs of corporate capital.

Marx's understandings are so fundamentally embedded in the bones and fabric of contemporary life we can only pretend to wish him or them away. To state this is not so much a political or ideological statement as much as it is a recognition of the place of Marx in everyday life, in much the same way as we might recognize the continuing legacy of Darwin or Freud. But such a statement does recognize the power of contemporary ideology to shut Marx's thought out of our consciousness. Often those who want to transcend or discard original thinkers the most quickly are those most deeply influenced by them and most deeply committed to them.

Marx's analysis is based in the examination of the central tenets of capitalism's prevailing forces. Private ownership of the **modes of production**, the profit-taking that is central to capitalist accumulation, the legitimizing of class relationships and the resulting disparities—all these present both the material conditions and ideological formations that justify the continuation of the oppression of people within our societies. The exploitation and **commodification** of working people are maintained and justified under a canopy of capitalist ideology that militates against the perception of any possibilities for social justice, locally or globally. The continued exploitation of Third World peoples and resources is no less destructive; indeed, the capitalist system necessarily assumes the discarding of certain portions of the world's population. Economic disparity gains credibility within the new ideological formations of modern consumerism, which has become almost a new religion. The obsession to acquire goods fuels the flames of capitalist production: a growth model of production, increasingly technologically driven, endures while millions of people are unemployed and displaced around the world. Those advantaged by the commodification of all domains of human social life continue to reap the benefits provided by capitalism's inherent disparities.

The ideological hegemony that maintains both the modes of production and the ideological formations that justify them controls our thinking and acting and denies the development of counterarguments. Alternative possibilities are subsumed under modern forms of consumer appeasement. Given these tendencies, we need to distinguish between Marx's profoundly powerful analysis of society and the voluminous interpretations of his prescriptions. Our work here, recognizing the embeddedness of Marx's thought, also stresses the need to continue to reveal and illuminate his contribution to social analysis—and not least because of its false burial.

The Marxist perspective has both historical and contemporary moments, each with a different explanatory power in present society. From our point of view, the early historical moments of Marx's dialectical materialism are fundamental. In response to Hegel's dialectical **idealism**, which proposed that historical change and progress were the result of contradictions within ideas, Marx's materialist perspective situated historical movement within the lived social and economic relationships of people. In recognizing how economic relationships condition or determine the dimensions of peoples' everyday lives, Marx understood how the structure of peoples' relationships to each other and to the larger systems within the economy worked.

Marx's theoretical position proposes an understanding of power and people's relationships to power structures by showing that power, advantage and disadvantage, and privilege and poverty are fundamentally governed by people's relationship to the modes of production, to the economy. In other words, the work we do, the income we create for ourselves, the economic structure of our communities—all of these conditions shape our everyday lives and determine our economic and social well-being. They shape the possibilities of life.

But what is production at this point in history, when one work site after another has been automated? What does it mean to have economic advantage or disadvantage? Under capitalism, relationships are structured to the advantage of some and the disadvantage of others. Power relationships shift within the economic/technical matrix and according to the resources available in any particular historical period. Under the current phase of **globalization**, many industrialized and less industrialized societies are witnessing a major social and economic restructuring. States are pushing towards **privatization** and **deregulation** of public institutions such as health care and transportation industries and also towards a reduction in public expenditures. Decisions regarding public policy and the public funding of such policies emerge out of political and ideological perspectives that tend to support the positions of those who are already advantaged.

To deepen our understanding of these developments, Marx's materialist perspective examines the distinction between the forces of production—the material resources historically available and the scientific organization of production and labour—and the relations of production—the distributive mechanisms of income and wealth as related to production and the recognition of the class structure, which is an expression of these relationships. The productive relationships themselves, which define the economic contexts of society and vary historically within capitalist economies, determine the emergent idea structures: the political, religious, and legal formulations that control and influence how people relate to and think about their social lives. As Marx suggests:

> In the social production of their life, men enter into definite relations that are indispensable and independent of their will, relations of production which correspond to a definite stage of development of their material productive forces. The sum total of these relations of production constitute the economic structure of society, the real foun-

dations, on which rises a legal and political superstructure and to which correspond definite forms of consciousness. The mode of production in material life conditions the social, political and intellectual life processes in general. It is not the consciousness of men that determine their being, but on the contrary, their social being that determines their consciousness. (McLellan, 1977: 389)

An historical example that clearly illustrates this relationship is a comparative look at the First Nations people of the prairies and those of the Pacific Northwest. The economic resource base of the prairie buffalo led to the emergence of certain social/cultural/artistic formations that were distinctly different from those that arose out of the economic resource base of the Pacific's salmon and cedar. To satisfy the needs of shelter, for example, the resource base of one society led to the development of the teepee; the other led to the longhouse.

In its analysis of the relationship between the material/economic lives of people and the overriding idea formations that influence people's conceptualizations, Marx's framework takes us into an exploration of social structures and personal experience. It presents us with a context for analysis of contemporary economic conditions as well as the ideological frames that emerge out of them. But Marx also pointed to another fundamental dynamic that controls and influences the experiences of individuals within society and has power both at the macrolevel and the microlevel: the distinction between *the state* and what he called **civil society** (see Marx, 1970a).

Today the state is often superficially perceived as an entity pertaining to government and often, within that understanding, as referring only to the people elected to form a government. This limited view does not adequately explain the full place and power of the state in the relations of everyday life. As Sylvia Hale points out, "The state itself is not an entity but rather is a process, comprising multiple elements. It includes federal, provincial, and local governments, parliamentary assemblies, the civil service, the military, the police, the judiciary, and a range of other supporting institutions" (Hale, 1995: 267; see also Glenday and Duffy, 1994: 127). Similarly—but taking this range of meaning somewhat further—some theorists use the term **state apparatus** (Althusser, 1969) to include the various bureaucracies and educational and health systems that make up the state. The term "apparatus" has conceptual power in that it recognizes the state as an array of practices, arrangements, and structures. As Nicos Poulantzas explains:

> If the state in the imperialist metropolises, though at present undergoing certain modifications, still maintains its character as a national state, this is due among other things to the fact that the state is not a mere tool or instrument of the dominant classes, to be manipulated at will, so that every step that capital took towards internationalization would automatically induce a parallel "supranationalization" of states. The task of the state is to maintain the unity and cohesion of a social formation divided into classes, and it focuses and epitomizes the class contradictions of the whole social formation in such a way as to sanction and legitimize the interests of the dominant classes and fractions as against the other classes of the formation, in the context of world class contradictions. (Poulantzas, 1975: 78)

Counterpointed with the concept of the state is the idea of civil society: the sites within our work lives, family lives, and communities. As Roberta Hamilton notes:

> In the neo-Marxist conception, the state is not a set of institutions with discrete functions, but rather a dense network of relations that are informed by the same struggles over the political meanings and goals that are occurring throughout society. These struggles are about everything from competition for support from different kinds of capital, to the form and substance of the welfare state, to the debates over curricula in the schools and universities. From this perspective, what falls outside the state—which does not mean that it is impervious to its influences—is called *civil society*: familial and household relationships, labour unions, churches, voluntary associations, and political parties. Whether or how a concern or demand within civil society is taken up within the state is highly variable and complex. (Hamilton, 1996: 103)

This is the domain of society that Jeremy Rifkin (1995) calls the "third sector," in counterdistinction to the "public sector" or the "private sector." Some commentators see civil society as the intermediary between the family and the state. In questioning the role of the state within this wider understanding, we see that the continuing separation of the state from civil society is a fundamentally contested zone within contemporary political life. Glenday and Duffy ask the following question in setting this relationship: "*Is the state the people's advocate, neutral mediator or corporate ally?*" (Glenday & Duffy, 1994: 117).

The need to analyze the place and power of the state in society as a whole has led to various theories of the state (see Knuttila, 1992; Pupo, 1994; Miliband, 1973; Panitch, 1997; Poulantzas, 1975, 1976). For our purposes, it is important to recognize that the state's place in our lives is both structural and experiential. Something as ordinary—and necessary—as a glass of water is a product of state regulation of sizeable complexity: there are rules and regulations governing what water sources can be used, how water should be treated, what pipes should be constructed from and where these pipes should be laid, the conditions for manufacturing and retailing standards of glassware, and so on. But on a much broader level the state controls the economic relationships of society from the manipulation of economic conditions for capital accumulation to legitimizing capitalist arrangements by way of extensive school curriculum presentations that validate existing social conditions. The state directs labour-market conditions, controls immigration, and intervenes in economic life in ways that often go unnoticed, such as the underwriting of corporate subsidies. The state also becomes an interpreter of this history. When people politically express the desire to dismantle the state, to get rid of big government—which means, subtextually, state intervention in the private sector—the invocation can have a false ring to it, especially when one reaches for a glass of water or remembers the e-coli water tragedy in Walkerton, Ontario, in May 2000.

The state also controls health care, both the services and the goods related to medical practice; it controls social welfare and assistance and intervenes in family life in a whole array of situations. One of the most significant themes to emerge out of the concept of the state and its relationship to the individual is the distinction between that which is public and that which is private, or what has come to be known as the **public/private divide** (see Boyd, 1997). The interpenetration at all levels of experience, in our daily lives, and in our larger understandings—for instance (to cite just one oft-used example), of what is taxable and what is not—compels us to question the nature of the state in our lives, both public and private.

In addition, under emergent globalized economic arrangements and liberalized free-trade agreements, the concept and the reality of the nation-state are coming under question. Are corporate entities organizing transnational, globalized economic and social policies in such a manner that the nation-state no longer has control of traditionally state-controlled aspects, such as investment, environmental regulation, social programs regulation, labour migration, or even the various dynamics of governance? The emergence of highly technical work environments—for example, the automation/robotization of jobs and the proliferation of part-time, casual jobs—raises additional questions. So-called globalized economic, political, and social realities raise two fundamental questions: Are we witnessing the end of the nation-state? And does capital still need labour? In other words, are workers needed at all? (On globalization, see Teeple, 1995, 2000; Barlow 1991, 1998; Clarke 1997; and Rifkin, 1995.) The answers to both of these questions provide an important key to our understanding of the ideological nature and the structures of the various dimensions of our daily lives.

Conclusion

In all of these considerations Mills's linkage of the personal to the public and Marx's materialist perspective provide essential guidelines to an understanding of ideology and the placement or displacement (decentring) of the state (see Magnusson, 1983)—as does Fatima Mernissi's personal and political story, which reveals much about the complex issues that people everywhere face in the intense moments of their everyday lives. The public/private space that she draws to our attention is situated within the ideological structures of her society. The key moments she describes make us aware of how her identity came into being—the forces, material and ideological, that shaped her identity. Analogous moments, of course, also emerge in our lives. These issues and questions will form the substance of the following chapters.

CHAPTER 2

Ideology:
Definitions, Representation, and Contextualization in Postmodernist Society

The word "ideology," one might say, is a *text*, woven of a whole tissue of different conceptual strands; it is traced through by divergent histories, and it is probably more important to assess what is valuable or can be discarded in each of these lineages than to merge them forcibly into some Grand Global Theory. (Eagleton, 1991: 1)

The term ideology has a wide range of historical meanings, all the way from the unworkably broad sense of the social determination of thought to the suspiciously narrow idea of the deployment of false ideas in the direct interests of a ruling class. Very often, it refers to the ways in which signs, meanings and values help to reproduce a dominant social power; but it can also denote any significant conjuncture between discourse and political interests. (Eagleton, 1991: 221)

Of all the terms used in the social sciences to help clarify social structure, social experience, and social theory, ideology is perhaps one of the most difficult to define. In a brief but profound manner in his book *Keywords*, a work he calls "historical semantics" (that is, **etymology**), Raymond Williams both establishes a framework for the term "ideology" and reveals its complexity. The word, he says, "first appeared in English in 1796, as a direct translation of the new French word *idéologie*, which had been proposed in that year by the rationalist philosopher Destutt de Tracy [1754–1836]" (Williams, 1976: 126). Tracy was, apparently, suggesting the term be used as a way of capturing the "philosophy of mind" or "science of ideas." The new term recognized the powerful place of ideas within the life of modern society.

Then, as Williams points out, in early nineteenth-century France the life of the word shifted dramatically. The French emperor Napoleon Bonaparte introduced a negative meaning to the terms ideology and "ideologues," attacking "the proponents of democracy—'who mislead the people by elevating them to a sovereignty which they were incapable of exercising'" (Williams, 1976: 126). In that sense, then, the term became synonymous with a form of mystification or false understanding, thus beginning its mixed career as a concept laden with "pejorative meaning" and moving far away from the original sense based on rational philosophy or science. The term's meaning quickly became contested, though certainly no less powerful in its implications.

Some 200 years later our rudimentary definition of ideology—closer to Napoleon's sense than to Destutt de Tracy's—touches on the central themes that rise out of various definitions: *an ideology is a set of beliefs that seems to serve and shape the interests of a certain group in society; has a legitimating/justifying function; and has the power to control or influence how people think about, or act in, their social circumstances.* Imagine for a moment a set of beliefs that serve your interests. Imagine that you share these beliefs with others in your life, your community, your culture. Imagine that, as a result of their shared dimension, the beliefs are seen as legitimate and recognized as having a public, not simply private, dimension. Imagine how these beliefs enforce, or reinforce, thoughts and actions within a specific time and place—a specific context. For example, in a discussion of forestry issues, an executive from a large forestry products corporation, a forester from a smaller company, a government forestry specialist, an environmentalist, a First Nations tribal councillor, or an interested citizen will most likely each bring a different system of thought and practice to the issues. Each has a viewpoint—a "standpoint," to use Dorothy Smith's expression (1977: 13). Each point of view sees forestry policy within its own ideological perspective.

At some point during such a discussion someone might say, "Time is money." This is a common saying, and it has an ideological significance. Its conceptual base has a social, economic, and political resonance in contemporary society. For many working people, their families, and their communities, the relationship between time and money in every-day life will have a different meaning than it might have, say, for a tele-marketing agent or a forestry company manager who has a contract to provide a certain amount of softwood lumber by a set deadline. For parents needing to provide for their children—to educate and nurture them—the time spent with those children will seldom, if ever, be based on any issues related to profit-potential.

Someone else in the forestry discussion might take the opportunity to remark, "The business of business is profit." That notion reflects a quite different view of working life than that held by someone who sees their vocation as "making a living," or contributing to their family's survival, or making a contribution to the needs of their community. A distinction has to be made between the moral/cultural domains and the economic domains of human life and societies, a distinction often hidden from view (see Teeple, 1995: 122). These hidden connections surface as contradictions, seen for instance when television mixes with religion and religion mixes with family life. The following example, from Kalle Lasn's book *Culture Jam*, makes the connection between the moral/reli-gious and the economic/business domains clear by pulling at the ideo-logical heart-strings of the nation:

> In a network TV ad for the Mormon Church some years ago, a little boy walks tentatively into a board-meeting-in-progress, a tableful of men in suits. He shuffles over to the fellow at the end of the table, peers up and says, "Dad, is time really worth money?" The room falls silent. The boy has his father's attention. "Why yes, Jimmy, it is." Whereupon the kid plunks his piggy bank down on the table. "Well, I'd like to play ball after dinner." (Lasn, 1999: 171)

Someone else might say, "Professionals have the expertise to look after their clients." Of course, expertise— indeed, the term professional itself— are not only related to knowledge, but also to secret knowledge or a struc-tured secrecy of knowledge. "Hard work will pay off," "if you want something done right, you have to do it yourself," "the squeaky wheel gets the grease"—all have ideological implications. One critic, John Fiske, argues that such clichés are the common-sense, everyday articulation of the dominant ideology:

> Indeed, the use of metaphors like "time is money," "spending or wasting time," or "investing time in" has become so clichéd that we tend to forget they are metaphors; they make time conform perfectly to the Protestant work ethic. What we get is a capitalist sense of time, in which time is turned into something that can be possessed, saved, or invested, something that some people can have more of than others, that can reward the efficient and penalize the lazy. The metaphor is fully hegemonic, it is common sense in performance as an ideological practice. (Fiske, 1989: 118)

These examples begin our articulation of certain words and ideas as ideologically based terms—as shorthand enclosures of ideas that have power to shape or control how we act in society. The ideological basis of our lives, the ideological background to our actions, is often either taken for granted or left below the level of explicit conscious awareness. Yet, the impact upon our daily lives is enormous and needs to be unambiguous if we are to examine ourselves, our experiences, our actions, and our relations with others in our communities with greater clarity and meaning. For example, what is the impact on ourselves and our communities when issues move from the public to the private domain, or vice versa, or when we allow greater state intervention into our lives or advocate for less state intervention? Should everyone be responsible for his or her own health care, or do we all have responsibility for health issues within communities?

These are not simply either/or issues. They form the background of our daily lives and influence how we act. Our ideological perceptions of events shape our interactions and commitments within our communities.

The Shaping of the Term "Ideology"

Self-Interested Justification

In their *Modern Dictionary of Sociology*, George A. Theodorson and Achilles Theodorson offer a definition of ideology that is seemingly both comprehensive and basic, yet complex. For them, an ideology is:

> a system of interdependent ideas (beliefs, traditions, principles, and myths) held by a social group of society, which reflects, rationalizes and defends its particular social, moral, religious, political, and economic institutional interests and commitments. Ideologies serve as logical and philosophical justifications for a group's patterns of behavior, as well as its attitudes, goals, and general life situation. (Theodorson & Theodorson, 1969: 195)

This definition alerts us to some of the themes that form adjacent structures or associated concepts to ideology and that, therefore, need to be explained and integrated into a full understanding. A number of key words and phrases drive the definition: "a system of interdependent ideas … held by a social group"; "reflects, rationalizes, defends"; the notion that ideologies are seen as "justifications" for specific interests. Significantly, without quite deserting Napoleon's attitude towards the concept of ideology, the Theodorsons' definition brings us closer to Destutt de Tracy's "science of ideas." Ideologies, in the meaning exhibited here, are partly a reflection of the social world of the group, a group which—through its everyday, lived experiences and ongoing structures and institutional formations—creates, maintains, and establishes ideas that "work" for it. These systems of ideas not only reflect but also rationalize and defend (that is, give justification for) the world the way it is, or at least how it is perceived to be within the social consciousness of the group. Indeed, it serves the interests of this group. Whose interests does the maxim "time is money" serve? Does it help in justifying capitalism or the business of profit-taking or profit-making in a highly professionalized, highly institutionalized society that favours the interests of capitalists over others?

Of particular importance here is the conceptualization of ideology as a reflection of, and as a fortification or legitimation for, a group's social life. In other words, the term has a dialectical quality. Ideologies both generate structures that shape our view and are generated within the structures and contexts of the society. Thus, we are socialized to certain ideologies and we are producers of ideologies within our daily lives.

How are ideologies integrated into our consciousness and our subconsciousness? As Patricia Marchak (1988: 2) notes, "Ideologies are screens through which we perceive the world.... They are seldom taught explicitly and systematically. They are rather transmitted through example, conversations, and casual observation." She provides the following example:

> The child asks the parent: "Why is that family poorer than us?" and receives an answer such as "Because their father is unemployed" or "Because sales clerks don't make as much money as sales managers." The accumulation of such responses provides a ready index to the organization of the society in occupational terms, and with reference to age and gender roles. The child is informed by such responses that some occupations provide higher material rewards than others, that an occupation is essential, and that fathers, not mothers, earn family incomes. The child is not provided with an explanation for the differential between sales clerks and sales managers, between the employed and the unemployed, between families in one income group and families in the other, but some children think to ask. There are, then, additional responses such as: "If you work hard at school, you can go to the top," or "Managers are more important than clerks," or "Well, if people don't work, they can't expect to get along in the world." (Marchak, 1988: 2)

This statement points to two ideas that are key to an understanding of the concept of ideology: first, the idea of *accumulation* — that ideological understandings accumulate over time in a continuous construction of conceptual and explanatory systems—and, second, that accumulation, in Marchak's words, "provides *a ready index to the organization of the society*" (our emphasis). Therefore, to speak of ideologies is not the same as to speak of values, norms, or the mores of a society. Ideologies (as the definition given in Chapter 1 indicates) are systems of values, systems of ideas. As Marchak's example illustrates, the ideological elements contained within certain phrases or strings of ideas engage us at a number of different levels of understanding, but if we want to unravel them or get at their root meanings, they also demand a diversity of analysis. Ideologies do, indeed, form a framework through which we see, comprehend, and act in our daily lives.

Below the Level of Consciousness

The noted French sociologist Louis Althusser offers a different approach to ideology, one that follows from what we have just discussed but that takes us to another level of analysis. In his work Althusser alerts us to a component of ideology not always noted: the distinction between consciousness and subconsciousness. "Ideology," he says, "has very little to do with 'consciousness.'" Rather, "it is profoundly unconscious":

> Ideology is indeed a system of representations, but in the majority of cases these representations have nothing to do with "consciousness": they are usually images and occasionally concepts, but it is above all as structures that they impose on the vast majority of men, not via their "consciousness." They are perceived-accepted-suffered cultural objects and they act functionally on men via a process that escapes them. (Althusser, 1969: 233)

According to this line of thought, although certain ideas lie below the surface of our consciousness, they govern our thoughts and our relationships with social representations and images in profound ways. Althusser also alerts us to the structural nature of ideological formations, but he neither psychologizes nor attempts to individualize the concept and does not attempt to suggest that it is simply or easily available to us. The structures of ideology penetrate and are embedded in consciousness, in part because of their power to do so without us knowing that this is, in fact, taking place.

Althusser's point is crucial: both the power of ideology and a recognition of its site in consciousness, often below our level of explicit awareness, carry major implications with regard to the development of critical consciousness and, indeed, for determining the possibilities of achieving social justice in a society.

"Isms" and the Sociology of Knowledge

Yet another definition of ideology builds on the array of meanings surrounding the term:

> The term has been used in three important senses: (1) to refer to very specific kinds of belief; (2) to refer to beliefs that are in some sense distorted or false; (3) to refer to any set of beliefs, covering everything from scientific knowledge, to religion, to everyday beliefs about proper conduct, irrespective of whether it is true or false. (Abercrombie, Hill, & Turner, 1988: 118)

The first component of this definition displays the most common understanding of ideology, indeed, the meaning given to it in most people's everyday experience. It is, in essence, what we might call the "political science perspective," the approach adopted and taught, for the most part, in North American academia. This approach takes in various ideologies such as democratic-liberalism, communism, and fascism, to name only a few. These are comprehensive belief systems that shape views of the world. They are normally integrated into public consciousness as forms of simple criticism or affirmation of political positions. In a very interesting way these formations, or at least people's positions regarding them, are also, once again, often located below the level of awareness—they remain at the taken-for-granted level of understanding. In other words, people may hold a particular ideological or political position, yet be unable to articulate the essential components that form it. The anti-communist rhetoric still prevalent today is an example of this tendency.

People hold or value certain ideological positions or have wholesale criticisms of them without necessarily comprehending all or even any of the underlying concepts that form the basis of the position. For example, when people say they want to "move beyond left and right politics," are they clear on the elements that make up those political positions that they want to move beyond? The statement assumes the existence of a political spectrum or continuum, with "the left" on one end and "the right" on the other. But are the people who make this suggestion clear on the various elements that form this spectrum? For example, how is **conservatism** distinct from **liberalism**? Are there moments of continuity between **socialism** and conservatism?

The Political Continuum

> I feel we're in a very shabby moment, and neither the literary nor the musical experience has its finger on the pulse of our crisis. We're in the midst of a Flood; and this Flood is of such enormous and Biblical proportions that I see everyone holding on in their individual way to an orange crate, to a piece of wood, and we're passing each other in this swollen river that has pretty well taken down all the landmarks, and overturned everything. And people insist, under these circum-stances, on describing themselves as liberal or conservative. It seems to me completely mad. (Cohen, 1999: C2)

In this passage, poet, novelist, and singer Leonard Cohen acknowledges the existence of a left-right continuum (though he only cites the conser-vative-liberal portions of it). But, oddly, he also denies its importance, or perhaps its usefulness, in this particular historical "shabby moment." According to him, we're all lost (and this includes "everyone," it seems), drifting in a flood, without a paddle. Indeed, most of us, like Cohen, tend to take "left" and "right" politics for granted, and many of us either don't want to place ourselves in that spectrum or have a hard time doing so—we don't want to pin ourselves down that way. But it can be a useful exercise for each of us to identify our own perspective or position on the political spectrum as well as to recognize the positions of others within our society.

⟵ socialism — liberalism — neo-liberalism — conservatism ⟶

The concept of "left wing" and "right wing" originated over two centuries ago, in the National Assembly in revolutionary France (1789–91), where the nobles sat on the president's right hand and the "commons" on the left. Within this horseshoe shape, then, the extremes of left and right sat closest to each other. At that point, the "left" had nothing to do with "socialism," a concept that only emerged in the following century. According to Williams, the concept of "liberal" appeared as early as the fourteenth century (in the meaning of "free man"), but like the other concepts "its political meaning is comparatively modern" (Williams, 1976: 148).

Significantly, certain of the key concepts—from socialism through liberalism to conservatism and **neo-conservatism** (also sometimes referred to as **neo-liberalism**)—establish dualities and create dialectic tensions in, for example, the relationships between the individual and the collectivity, freedom and determinism, the state and civil society, **ascribed status** and **achieved status**, scientific thought and religious thought, co-operation and competition, social change and status quo, the élite and the masses, public and private, and so on. (For more on the major ideological perspectives, see, for example, Resnick, 2000; Hiller, 1996; Bowers, 1987; and Shapiro, 1958.)

Socialism

Fundamental to this position on the continuum is a commonly understood recognition of both the importance of the collectivity—people acting together and sharing interests and resources in common—and the interests of the collectivity's needs in relationship to the individual. Adherents to this perspective also believe that social justice is a goal for all in society and that actions and policies that provide social justice will emerge from a more equitable distribution of wealth and knowledge in all levels and layers of society. Indeed, economic and/or material needs form the substructural basis for emergent ideas that form the superstructure (see Chapter 1, p. 16–17). In addition, the state has a fundamental obligation to play a major role in the maximization of social equality. The collective goals of the community must be respected, and the distribution of resources should serve the public good, not the private needs and interests of the élite. Another element in achieving social justice is the recognition of class interests and the gendered and ethnic class locations within society.

The socialist space on the spectrum takes in a wide variety of formations, from communism, Marxist-Leninism, and Trotskyism on the left to **democratic socialism** and—on the right side of the left space—**social democracy** (as represented in Canada by the New Democratic Party). The question most quickly raised by this distinction is "how far left are you?" Among those who contributed historically to the development of socialism are Claude H. Saint Simon (1760–1825) and, especially, Karl Marx (1818–83).

Liberalism

Liberalism—that is, liberalism with a lower case "l"—advocates an ethic of individualism, a perspective that reveres individual achievement or a meritocratic system of rewards. The English philosopher and economist John Stuart Mill (1806–73) was one of its early theorists. The liberal position emphasizes the individual's opportunity, unfettered by government intervention, to act as he or she wishes, without necessarily any collective concern for the common good. Although liberals do argue that people need to keep the good of others in mind, they maintain that the common good is best served by the freedom offered to the individual and the market. Their belief is that society's humanistic and economic goals can be reached—can find their most powerful expression—if thinking and action are based upon rational, scientific reason and scientific method.

In the twentieth century, liberalism as expressed within Western Europe and North America has advocated certain social programs, such as health care, public education, and a limited amount of social assistance—an approach that has been called Welfare state liberalism or liberal reformism. It emerged out of the work of English economist John Maynard Keynes (1883–1946), who recognized that the **free market** had often proved inadequate or, indeed, had "failed" to deliver the goods to all citizens. Liberal reformism, therefore, called for the intervention of the state to moderate the economic cycle. Some critics argue that the liberal advocacy of these programs amounts to a compromise symptomatic of "bleeding heartism" rather than a true commitment to the needs of the common good.

Liberalism seems always caught in the centre, on the fence, in danger of tottering towards the left or the right. Certainly, the mainstream brand of liberalism has to be differentiated from the more right-wing classical liberalism—that is, neo-conservatism or, as it has more recently been known, neo-liberalism. (Note also that the lower case "l" for liberalism is, of course, significant in distinguishing the philosophical/political understanding of liberalism from the political party, the Liberals.)

Neo-liberalism, Neo-conservatism, and Classical Liberalism

The work of the evolutionary philosopher Herbert Spencer (1820–1903) lies at the root of "neo-liberalism" (which sprang from "classical liberalism" and is sometimes also called "neo-conservatism"). Spencer, a believer in evolution before Darwin popularized the notion, brought together biology, psychology, sociology, and ethics in his nine-volume book *System of Synthetic Philosophy* (1862–93). His advocacy of **Social Darwinism**—the idea of "survival of the fittest" as applied to people rather than plants or animals—contributed to the core philosophical, as well as economic, perspective of neo-liberalism. Other theorists of this approach are the American economist Milton Friedman (b. 1912)—who has argued, for instance, that high incomes are a reward for taking risks—and Friedrich von Hayek (1899–1992), sometimes called "the father of monetarism."

This approach sees competition, rather than co-operation, as the driving force of social and economic conditions and change. In recent decades it has emphasized an opposition to state intervention in the economy, which in turn means deregulation and privatization (in brief, the three Ds: downsize, deregulate, decentralize). "Get the state/government out of the way" of free-enterprise, free-market, "laissez-faire" capitalism, its advocates say. A central ideological imperative of this position is the **ideology of individualism,** or individual freedom: the idea that whether a person wins or loses, is a success or a failure, depends on individual initiative and energy.

When people talk about "the right" or the "right-wing agenda" they are probably referring to this perspective. Sometimes the approach is referred to as neo-conservatism, which raises a problem of nomenclature.

The recent incarnations of this ideological approach—as seen in the administrations of Margaret Thatcher in the United Kingdom (first elected 1978), Ronald Reagan in the United States (1980), and Brian Mulroney in Canada (1984), as well as in the approach of provincial governments in Canada (the Progressive Conservatives in Alberta and Ontario) and in the programs of the federal Opposition Party, the Canadian Alliance — seem to drift far afield from the traditions of the conservative perspective and cannot really be described as a "new" version of conservatism. "Neo-liberalism" is the more appropriate label.

Conservatism

Most commonly, the conservative position recognizes the authority of tradition and the maintenance of the status quo. People who call themselves "conservative" generally see social inequalities as inevitable, indeed, as necessary as well as inevitable. Ascribed status has precedence over achieved status; privilege comes from home; the moral authority of religion is primal. The natural order of society has a kind of fly-wheel momentum that economically, politically, and morally needs to be continued.

A certain dynamic within conservatism also maintains a tension between the community and the individual; the authority of religion or an adherence to a sense of common good, for instance, can mix with, and somewhat clash with, aims to satisfy or stabilize the needs and the well-being of the individual. An early theorist of this position is the British statesman and political philosopher Edmund Burke (1729–97).

In recent times the conservative tradition has been largely neglected, which is odd because this particular space on the continuum has had a solid historical impact in North America as the home of cultural, religious, and ethnic groups desiring self-determination and the protection of their traditions. It can also be perceived as the place for ecological or environmental groups, who are trying to conserve the environment. Ironically, within the Canadian context, socialists can find themselves cast as conservatives when they defend and work to preserve a half-century of moderate social programs.

One final note, which might be applied to more than one of the ideological positions on the continuum, relates to the term "radical." This complicated term, which essentially derives from the meaning "of the root or roots," is often used in the realm of left politics, where someone who is radical might call for far-reaching change or want to get to the roots of things, but historically—and currently—it has also been applied to the radical right, to people who are also seeking fundamental change, though of a quite different order, "as distinct from a more conventional conservatism" (Williams, 1976: 251).

In conclusion, what the elements of this continuum from left to right reveal is that these taken-for-granted philosophical and political frameworks are still very much with us today in popular discourse. The celebration of the "death of...," "the end of...," or the call to "move beyond..." are in themselves a form of masking ideological realities.

Back to "Isms"

The second component of Abercrombie, Hill, and Turner's definition of ideology—"to refer to beliefs that are in some sense distorted or false" (see above, p. 29) a position that arises from Marxist literature. It also moves us to one of the most important or most powerful understandings of the term, explored by Karl Marx and Friedrich Engels in *The German Ideology* (1970). As Williams (1976: 127) notes, the Marx and Engels presentation of ideology seems to have a certain continuity with Napoleon's pejorative sense of the term: ideology is false knowledge or half-truths. Interestingly, Marx's powerful term **false consciousness** is an outcome of what he sees as mystified, interested knowledge that serves the capitalist class while falsifying the knowledge and understanding of the disadvantaged.

Marx and Engels outline the essential distinction between ideological knowledge and scientific knowledge. For them, scientific knowledge is derived from the lived experience of people in real circumstances, not from concepts abstracted from or laid on to people's lived experiences (see Smith, 1990: 31). On the other hand, abstracted, false, or illusory knowledge is ideology. These false or distorted forms of ideas serve or justify positions of specific advantage.

In addition, Marx and Engels pinpoint the self-interested nature of knowledge, particularly as it is constructed by the ruling class: "The ideas of the ruling class are in every epoch the ruling ideas, i.e., the class which is the ruling *material* force of society, is at the same time the ruling *intellectual* force"(Marx and Engels, 1970: 64; emphasis in original). The idea of this self-interested nature of knowledge is, as we will see, connected to the perspective of the sociology of knowledge.

Much of the work developed by Marx and Engels in their treatise on ideology is in conflict with, though derivative of, the concept of "German ideology" theorized by the German philosopher Georg Hegel (1770–1831). Their argument presents the confrontation of the idealist, Hegelian perspective with that of a materialist perspective. For Marx, the history of societies is not the abstract history of ideas but the sensuous, lived history of people in their concrete, everyday social and economic experience. Marx and Engels explore the actions of people in making or constructing knowledge; they look at how, in people's daily practices of comprehending or apprehending social relations, knowledge becomes an ideological, rather than a scientific, construction. Within complex societies a process of falsification takes place.

The German Ideology presents **three tricks** by which knowledge is distorted into ideology to serve the interests of the élite:

1. Ideological formulations separate the ideas of a particular epoch from the individuals who form the ruling élite of that epoch and who have, indeed, created those ideas. In other words, dominant ideas become separated from the empirical reality that created them.

2. The ideas are established as part of an order that builds "mystical connections" among those same ideas; the connections, therefore, appear as though they are "real" rather than manufactured.

3. The ideas or concepts then must be taken up and solidified, or adapted, by theorists or advocates who represent them in history; that is, the "'thinkers,' the 'philosophers,' the ideologists, who are again understood as the manufacturers of history." (Marx & Engels, 1970: 67).

These three tricks follow an intricate process whereby knowledge or images of reality are transformed into formulations that alter or shift the meaning-structures of social events and circumstances. These processes of transformation are ultimately related to power, and in people's lived experience they create and destroy advantage. Therefore, Marx and Engels see ideological formations as false knowledge or half-truths—illusions created to mystify rather than knowledge intended to build understanding, much less to develop a critical consciousness. For example, a common belief in capitalist society is that a private business enterprise does not function only as a profit-making venture but also contributes to the development of community life and general well-being. In fact, it could be argued that the opposite is true: to ensure that they make a profit—the necessary condition of doing business in a capitalist society—most if not all businesses, when it comes to the "Bottom Line," have to leave aside considerations of the common good. Companies decide, for instance, to pay minimum wages (or wages as low as possible), to lay off workers, and to disregard environmental conditions as a necessary condition not just of staying in business but of earning maximum profits. Any altruism expressed, however sincere, is a false front in terms of the necessary business strategy for survival. Sometimes, donations by businesses to local charities or events are often part of a tax strategy, something contributing to that "Bottom Line." How does this false altruism get masked so easily within our society? Why did British Columbians, for instance, believe that business magnate Jimmy Pattison was "giving his time for a dollar" to sit as chair of the world's fair, Expo '86, in Vancouver? While he was giving his time, his corporate interests were profiting from the Expo developments. The "mystical connections" prevailed. Pattison was perceived as an altruistic spirit in the midst of tycoon capitalism around the world. At the same time, the BC Teachers Federation could not persuade the provincial government to institute a "poverty" curriculum that would inform their students about the plight of those parts of the province not included in the Expo "boom."

The process of image-making, illusion creation, and masking of social realities connects to another fundamental concept related to the domain of ideology: representation. How are certain groups within society advantaged, or disadvantaged, by the processes of ideological formation? Thus, the third component of Abercrombie, Hill, and Turner's definition of ideology develops from the sociology of knowledge, a domain of study rich in argument and understanding. It lies at the root of many other studies of society because of its exploration not only of the genesis of knowledge but also of its power, significance, and distribution in daily life. Although it may appear to be esoteric, the field is, in effect, the substratum of most studies of the social world. The sociology of knowledge has its roots in the theoretical formulations of Marx and Engels and in the major work of Karl Mannheim, *Ideology and Utopia*.

According to Marx, the ideological formations of a society (the superstructure) arise out of the material relations of production (the substructure). Given that the ruling class owns the modes of production as well as the means of mental production, again we are reminded about how "the ideas of the ruling class are in every epoch the ruling ideas" (Marx and Engels, 1970: 64). Mannheim further developed these Marxian concepts. He explored the notion that knowledge is created out of social interest or specific social contexts regardless of social class. This perspective recognizes a form of **relativism** regarding truth and knowledge. If all knowledge arises out of a particular social interest, then all knowledge is ideological. The political, social, and economic implications of this point of view are enormous. According to Mannheim: "The principal thesis of the sociology of knowledge is that there are modes of thought which cannot be adequately understood as long as their social origins are obscured" (Mannheim, 1936: 2). In the same way that those interested in the genesis of words want to discover or uncover the origin of their meanings, so, too, do those interested in the systems of ideas, words, and actions that form our ideological milieu desire some deeper or greater understanding of the starting point or origin of these complex influences upon our lives.

From Marx to Mannheim to Michael Jordan may seem a big leap, but there is a connection in our pursuit of the origins of popular meanings and knowledge. Basketball superstar Michael Jordan became a sports phenomenon—five times a league Most Valuable Player and a record nine scoring titles, among other accomplishments—and over his career became almost synonymous with the game and a major contributor to the game's massive growth in popularity, particularly among African-American youth (though he was equally popular with the White mainstream). The result, though, was not just an athletic "phenom" but a commercially driven spectacle, a meteoric development of associations. Michael Jordan himself became an icon of African-American success, achievement, and physical prowess, and in the popular, especially youthful, mind, the basketball shoes and other accessories with which he was associated became synonymous with personal identity. In the process the continual self-interested image-making of the contemporary athlete became perfectly combined with the ubiquitous sale of athletic wear and its advertising: an ideological formation.

In all of this, Jordan's basketball career becomes part of the structure of everyday life as well as a relentlessly driven commerce. As we explore the generation and fabrication of ideological formations, we must recognize that we have begun to build a way of knowing that essentially arises out of our ways of doing things in a capitalist society. Michel Foucault's use of the term "discourse" is useful here (see Foucault, 1972). From Foucault's perspective, discourse not only refers to words or communicative signs but also to language forms and practices that emerge out of the expressions that serve to structure our everyday lives, in part by placing our practice—our actions and thoughts—within specific contexts. These everyday practices and thoughts are "boundaried"; they are placed within enclosures that maintain the secrecy of the expert while controlling the interpretation received by the public.

A case in point is the genesis of Western medicine (the escalation of scientific practices that are exclusive rather than inclusive) and the formulations of knowledge and discourses surrounding its practice. Throughout history, drugs have been used to heal and mediate pain. At one time they were freely available—found in one's back yard, so to speak, or in the forest over yonder. Today, in the institutional structure of Western medicine—the health care complex, including hospitals, clinics, laboratories, and all their attendant professionals—drugs are bought and sold, and pharmaceutical companies occupy an exalted position. These days, in medical office waiting rooms, one sees not only patients but often a neatly dressed man (rarely a woman) holding a large black pharmaceutical supplies case. If one has a relatively simple health complaint, the doctor may reach into a desk drawer and offer a sample supply of some medication, left behind by such a salesman. In the application of drugs in Western medicine, interested knowledge emerges as scientifically and commercially or corporately based knowledge. The economic base out of which this knowledge emerges is often obscured or left unaddressed, especially from the point of view of the average citizen.

Mannheim states: "the sociology of knowledge seeks to comprehend thought in the concrete setting of an historical-social situation out of which individually differentiated thought only very gradually emerges" (Mannheim, 1936: 3). This conceptualization of the "gradual emergence" of our thoughts and actions, our ways of knowing, acting, and being recognizes what Marchak has referred to as the accumulated, ready indexes of the organization of society. The emergence of knowledge is often slow or incremental, but our common comprehension is nonetheless clearly shared. The "phenomenon" turns into a "phenom" whether as sports celebrity or the surgeon as shaman.

Mannheim's perspective raises significant and difficult questions regarding knowledge as a relative matter (relativism). Is all knowledge socially interested and, therefore, based on perspective? Is all knowledge relative to a specific context? Are there no eternal truths? If this is so, how is power to be distributed or legitimized, and who is to determine this?

Mannheim contrasts relativism with the concept of relationism near the end of his major work:

> Just as the fact that every measurement in space hinges upon the nature of light does not mean that our measurements are arbitrary, but merely that they are only valid in relation to the nature of light, so in the same way not relativism in the sense of arbitrariness but relationism applies to our discussions. Relationism does not signify that there are no criteria of rightness and wrongness in a discussion. It does insist, however, that it lies in the nature of certain assertions that they cannot be formulated absolutely, but only in terms of the perspective of a given situation. (Mannheim, 1936: 283)

Certainly, as we move beyond the definition of ideology into other matters related to the task of understanding its role and implications, we must take with us the elegance of its complexity. In both contemporary academic and non-academic discourse, ideology is understood in three ways:

1. perhaps most commonly, ideology is an "...ism"—socialism, liberalism, conservatism;
2. ideology is distorted truth, a half-truth—serving the interests of powerful, advantaged groups within societies; and
3. ideology can refer to all forms of knowledge—in the sense that all knowledge emerges out of specific interests.

Most commonly, when people comment that some expression or utterance is ideological, they are applying the second understanding of the term, which is the Marxist rendering. Our use of the term recognizes that ideology refers to knowledge that emerges socially, culturally, and historically from specific social and economic contexts. Therefore, we need to investigate the origins of ideas if we are not to be controlled or victimized by them. As with all discourse, our endeavours in this regard need to consider what meanings people have attached to the terms of reference that they use—or, indeed, if they have even thought about these meanings when using the terms.

Representation

Stuart Hall, in *Representation: Cultural Representations and Signifying Practices*, uses the *Shorter Oxford English Dictionary* to provide a definition of his key term:

1. To represent something is to describe or depict it, or call it up in the mind by description or portrayal or imagination; to place a likeness of it before us in our mind or in the senses; as for example, "This picture represents the murder of Abel by Cain."
2. To represent also means to symbolize, stand for, to be a specimen

of, or to substitute for; as in the sentence, "In Christianity, the cross represents the suffering and crucifixion of Christ." (Hall, 1997: 16)

Leaving aside the Judeo-Christian ideological dynamics embedded within these definitions (definition by example is always situated in a particular context), we can see that representation involves, first, the process of construction of ideologies and the subsequent representation of them within the cultural, political, and social dimensions of archaic as well as modern society. This condition, following Marx and Engels, includes the distorted forms of communication that become structured into ideological realities and that are particularly evident in the historical construction of various ethnic relationships and representations that form the basis of racist attitudes (see Henry, 2000; James, 1999; Satzewich, 1998; Li & Bolaria, 1988). The stereotyping of certain social groups emerges out of the socially constructed representations of these groups, generated by current ideological systems. **People of colour** experience this phenomenon on a daily basis in their relationships with such social institutions as the schools and the police.

Secondly, representations form a fundamental substratum within which the images of how the world works or how people should act in a larger sense become embodied. For example, although media representations of a particular ethnic group may be accurate or inaccurate, they all the same become part of the social representation of the group, that is, part of both the prevailing public presentation and the conceptual schema that forms how the public makes sense of the group and eventually relates to it. In his book *Orientalism*, Edward Said provides an example of how constructed representations can become the public's only way of understanding a particular group. He explores how the Orient, particularly Islam, has been constructed by Westerners as Other (different, inferior) in relation to the Occident (superior) and how people in both the East and West have internalized the ideology of Orientalism. Whether the representations are correct or incorrect, they remain the public's only code of reference. As Said states:

> Islam *has* been fundamentally misrepresented in the West—the issue
> is whether indeed there can be a true representation of anything, or

whether any and all representations, because they *are* representations, are embedded first in the language and then in the culture, institutions, and political ambience of the representer. If the latter alternative is the correct one (as I believe it is), then we must be prepared to accept the fact that a representation is *eo ipso* implicated, intertwined, embedded, interwoven with a great many other things besides the "truth," which is itself a representation. (Said, 1979: 252)

In his later work *Covering Islam*, Said (1981) takes the issue of representation and its impact much further. He discusses how various Western academics, governments, and media construct misrepresentations of the Islamic world, in effect influencing how we see and react to that world. The repercussions of these representations were played out dramatically in the West after the events of September 11, 2001, when racial profiling (at least partially based on these representations) rapidly became more normalized. Some Western countries began passing new laws or resurrecting old ones to deal with the situation.

To conclude our discussion of representation, let us consider the work of Emile Durkheim (1858–1917), particularly his presentation regarding the notion of "concept" in *The Elementary Forms of Religious Life*. There he reveals some of the roots of the term representation or, as he expressed it, collective representations:

> The nature of the concept, thus defined, bespeaks its origin. If it is common to all, it is the work of the community. Since it bears the mark of no particular mind, it is clear that it was elaborated by a unique intelligence, where all others meet each other, and after a fashion, come to nourish themselves. If it has more stability than sensations or images, it is because collective representations are more stable than the individual ones; for while an individual is conscious even of the slight changes which take place in his environment, only events of a greater gravity can succeed in affecting the mental status of a society. Every time that we are in the presence of a type of thought or action which is imposed uniformly upon particular wills or intelligences, this pressure exercised over the individual betrays the intervention of the group. (Durkheim, 1912: 482)

He goes on to note how language "is the product of collective elaboration":

> Thus there is a great deal of knowledge condensed in the word which
> I never collected, and which is not individual; it even surpasses me to
> such an extent that I cannot even completely appropriate all its results.
> Which of us knows all the words of the language he speaks and the
> entire signification of each? (Durkheim, 1912: 482–83)

Contemporary thinkers and social theorists have come to new formulations of the problematics of representations that hold public power and currency. In *Voltaire's Bastards: The Dictatorship of Reason in the West*, John Ralston Saul traces the adoption of modern technocratic, business management perspectives to a growth of amorality. The techniques of the "Business School," he says, lead to a withering of "imagination, creativity, moral balance, knowledge, common sense, a social view" and to a growth of "competitiveness" and people who always have "an ever-ready answer, a talent for manipulating situations." The general result, above all else, he says, "is the growth of an undisciplined form of self-interest, in which winning is what counts."

> Such sudden respectability for undisciplined self-interest is one of the
> most surprising developments of the last three decades. It seems to
> indicate just how confused our society has become. In two and a half
> thousand years of Western social history, one of the very few things
> that most societies have agreed upon is that individual restraint is
> central to any civilization. (Saul, 1993: 121–22)

Therefore, by placing ideology within the forms of representation that hold public power and currency, regardless of how seemingly individualized they may have become, we can see the impact that these formations have upon the development of thought and action in contemporary society. This leads us to the dynamic of contextualization.

Contextualization

Any study of society has specific as well as generic moments. Much of the literature regarding inequality, or distribution of advantage, in contemporary society is explored within the complex of relationships undergirded by gender, ethnicity/race, and class. Indeed, given these relationships, we understand that such matters as economic policies, social policies, political platforms, and immigration policies carry advantages or disadvantages for some social group. The idea of contextualization demands that we keep these three fundamental categories—gender, race, and class—in mind; they form the grounded framework for our work.

Marx, again, provides an important point of departure regarding the notion of contextualization; that is, in order to comprehend the power, impact, or central dynamic of a particular social, economic, or political reality, we must situate it methodologically within its historical moment. To contextualize something is, in some very important way, to render it holistic, to develop a relational analysis of a particular element or event. To set in context is to see the relationships that surround a particular event or mechanism.

For example, Frances Henry and her co-authors, in their discussion of the ideology of **racism**, provide an example of how ideology acts in our everyday social lives. Articulating contextualization and racism in a manner that extends these concepts and connects them to idea, thought, attitude, action, and the lived social realities of everyday life, they quote Stuart Hall:

> Racism is not a natural element in society, just waiting for a series of events to trigger its manifestations: It has no natural and universal law of development. It does not always assume the same shape. There have been many significantly different racisms—each historically specific and articulated in a different way.... Racism is always historically specific in this way, whatever common features it may appear to share with other similar social phenomena.... It always assumes specific forms which arise out of the present—not the past—conditions and organization of society. (Hall, 1978: 26, quoted in Henry et al., 1995: 15)

Racism arises out of concrete social and economic contexts. The process of **racialization**, a term commonly used in the work on ethnicity and racism, refers to giving race centrality within social interpretations, to expressing an overtly ideological dynamic. Stephen Small (in Satzewich, 1998: 71–72), for example, writes about "racialized groups ... racialized barriers and hostilities ... and racialized identities." What he calls the "racialization problematic" is an ideologically driven comprehension of action, thought, and practice within our societies. Racialization is process-generated and driven by a deeply ideological current, but people become racialized within concrete social contexts. Certain ethnic groups have been identified according to an assumed phenotype to the extent that they have become essentialized. With the current war on terrorism, the practice of racial profiling in the United States has been expanded to include people of Middle Eastern origin.

In addition to these concepts of representation and contextualization, the term "postmodernism" also plays into an understanding of ideology. As Judy Rebick suggests in her book *Imagine Democracy*, the contemporary time and trend might best be characterized by the term "postmodern feudalism" (Rebick, 2000: 3).

On Postmodernism

The complex term postmodernism has its origins in the fields of art and architecture but more recently has been taken up as a catch-all concept heralding the transcendence of established "modern" forms and covering a wide range of disparate elements of contemporary social reality, including authority, **legitimacy**, and rationality. The term characterizes a society that is fragmented, with a multiplicity of identities, in which the canon of science and other forms of legitimacy and authority are open to question.

Postmodernism describes both a way of comprehending society—in other words, a theoretical conceptualization or framework for description—and a style, a form of artistic, literary, and architectural expression within society. The fragmented society it describes is one filled with a diversity of expression and perspective, a society in which no particular authority seems to have legitimacy or currency. Yet, at the same time that we observe this disintegration of commonality or agreement within society, we live in a world of increasing homogenization: "McDonaldization," as Ritzer (1993) calls it, a world of incipient "monoculture" according to Shiva (1997). Postmodernism is a conundrum. For example, within the field of health or health care, contradictions emerge. The envelope of Western medicine, characterized by the rationalization and technologization of medical practices, is challenged by alternatives such as acupuncture, homeopathy, and naturopathy. In politics, people whose policies and programs appear to be located on entirely different ends of the political spectrum align to form coalitions of agreement, forces riddled with what appear to be contradictions, yet in which they find a mono-causal moment of continuity. In the vast, nebulous world of "Internet knowledge," where is the authority or the site for establishing legitimacy? If everything is given currency, how do we identify or make judgments about quality? How do we establish a standard of morality or normative structure?

For young people, consciously or not, the ethos of postmodernism can become both a way of comprehending the world and a style. It can be a method of explanation (both academic and commonsensical) and a concrete form of dress or expression. For example, the television experience—the view, the "gaze," the enveloped mindset—blankets young people with advertising and programming that directly or indirectly sells such things as alcohol, sex, the idea (if not the reality) of owning fast cars and, of course, consuming fast food, and violence as a means of problem-solving, while these same experiences or driven needs may well be contested immoralities elsewhere in life, perhaps both at home and school. The contradictions, legitimacies, and illegitimacies of these moments of experience often find little or no explanation—there is no touchstone of authority to which young people, parents, teachers, or police, among others, can defer or find meaning. At one moment, "Anything goes!" "Just do it!" At the next, a young person is held accountable by a court of law whose standards of legitimacy would ravage those responsible for most of TV's advertising and programming if they were equally applied to them.

We all live with and within these inner identity formations—the multiplicity of identities or "selves" that we present to the world. We must constantly struggle to comprehend the meanings we are projecting or, sometimes, we struggle to avoid comprehending them. We internalize these meanings based on our social, cultural, political, and economic surroundings—the ideologies, the representations, the contexts. A singularity of identity, the concept of a monolithic self, has become less and less the norm for many people around the globe, but particularly within the urban, globalized communities of the world. We see, for instance, on a street in Vancouver a 16-year-old boy wearing a Nike "swoosh" designer hat, a Washington Redskins football jersey, Toronto Raptor basketball shorts, and Reebok running shoes, and walking by a Second Cup coffee emporium that has the graffiti "Fuck You" in orange spray paint adorning its canvas deck borders. Our everyday lives are saturated with signs and a multiplicity of symbol systems.

Postmodernist sense-making, like the various interpretations of the term ideology, involves a number of political domains and representational perspectives, all living within contexts of great complexity. Mike Featherstone outlines the "main features" of postmodernism:

> *First*, a movement away from the universalistic ambitions of master-narratives where the emphasis is upon totality, system and unity towards an emphasis upon local knowledge, fragmentation, syncretism, "**otherness**" and "difference." *Second*, a dissolution of symbolic hierarchies which entail canonical judgements of taste and value, towards a popular collapse of the distinction between high and popular culture. *Third*, a tendency towards the aestheticization of everyday life which gained momentum both from efforts within the arts to collapse the boundary between art and life (pop art, Dada, surrealism, and so on) and the alleged movement towards a simulational consumer culture in which an endlessly reduplicated hallucinatory veil of images effaces the distinction between appearance and reality. *Fourth*, a decentring of the subject, whose sense of identity and biographical continuity give way to fragmentation and superficial play with images, sensations and "multi-phrenic intensities" ... [a] bombardment of fragmented signs and images which erode all continuity between past, present and future. ... In opposition to the notion that life is a meaningful proj-

ect, here we have the view that the individual's primary mode of orientation is an aesthetic one. (Featherstone, 1995: 43–44)

Featherstone's presentation, itself, seems postmodernist, almost poetic: "fragmentation ... 'otherness' and 'difference' ... dissolution ... canonical judgements ... collapse of the distinction between high and popular culture ... aestheticization of everyday life ... towards a simulational consumer culture ... a decentring of the subject ... identity and biographical continuity give way to fragmentation." How to judge Mick Jagger against Mozart? The choices are infinite; the illusions of choices are even more infinite. Choices without context become merely gimmicks. Or do they?

Given these themes, from what source comes the signposts for our sense-making of modern or postmodern society? As Suzi Gablik writes, with particular reference to the artist:

> Everything is in continuous flux; there are no fixed goals or ideals that people can believe in, no tradition sufficiently enduring to avoid confusion. The legacy of modernism is that the artist stands alone. He has lost his shadow. As his art can find no direction from society, it must invent its own destiny. (Gablik, 1984: 13)

As in the image of the Canadian boy wearing a Nike hat or Fatima Mernissi's story of a Moroccan woman's clash over dress and gender within her family (see the quote at the beginning of Chapter 1), a number of questions arise. What do we need to do to invent our own identities? Do we all have to do so? What does this mean for society and its sense of direction? These questions and others like them also relate to the concept of socialization—how people come not just to fit into their society, but to know it and interpret it. They also lead to larger issues regarding the nature of power within public and private domains, within both our identities and our institutions or social communities.

Shared experiences are a key to this discussion, and as Varda Burstyn points out, "The rituals of sport engage more people in shared experience than any other institutional or cultural activity today. World Cup soccer gathers upwards of a billion electronic spectators on a global basis" (Burstyn, 1999: 33). The 2002 Olympic hockey finals had a similar effect in Canada.

The questions about the postmodern ethos and its social fragmentation, socialization, and power come into focus in the world of sport but are also evident in political relationships:

> Poststructuralist and postmodern theorists have argued that because the great master-narratives of the Enlightenment and modernism (rationalism, humanism, progress, liberalism, socialism) have lost their power to cohere society and individual identities, we are witnessing a multiplication of identities, and, with this, of masculinities in contemporary life.... Thinkers working within this perspective [postmodernism] are right to note the demise of many of the great modernist '-isms' in this period. [They] have done excellent work in detecting and sensitizing us to ways that individuals and communities have resisted prescriptive and oppressive ideologies within their cultures on a daily basis, and helped us understand the dynamics of subcultural community formation.
>
> However, the conditions of inequality that the modernist ideas sought to explain and address have not disappeared, despite vast changes in technology and consciousness. Financial, political, and military power is more concentrated today than at any other time in human history.... While many North Americans no longer believe politicians on either the left or right... this has not translated into a political radicalization, but rather to an overall conservatism, if that word can aptly be used to characterize the combination of mean-spirited individualism, patriarchal gender norms, and antisocial state policies evident in North American neoconservative political culture in the 1980s and 1990s. (Burstyn, 1999: 192–93)

Burstyn challenges us to reckon with the contradictions within our society that may be explained or interpreted too simplistically by the postmodernist perspective. She challenges the representation of fragmentation, flux, and mulitiplicity by demanding that we remember the material realities that we, and a huge part of the world, inhabit. She also raises another contradiction that emerges within the dynamics of this phenomenon—the potential for finding solace, security (both ideological and personal), and meaning within fundamentalism—which is essentially a form of literalism. The complexities involved in unravelling the social/economic/ political/cultural environment in which we live demand insight, energy, and, perhaps most certainly, the ability to live in ambiguity, open to the various layers of meaning that influence and play on and in our contemporary lives.

Conclusion

The glamour and stimulation of postmodernist cultural production, whether in sport or other forms of social experience, can mask the clarity we need to comprehend the dilemmas inherent in our societies. As we move further into the topic of ideology, we must engage the contradictions as they arise and steadfastly attempt to comprehend social reality within interpretations that examine the dialectic of diversity and monoculture that is so much a part of postmodernist culture.

CHAPTER 3

Socialization:
Awakening or Narcotic?

> Yet it can be argued that the difficulty in controlling the flow of new
> goods, images and information, which is generated by the modernist
> and market impulses within consumer societies, leads to *problems of*
> *misreading the [cultural] signs.* The problems we encounter in every-
> day practice because culture fails to provide us with a single taken-
> for-granted recipe for action introduces difficulties, mistakes and
> complexity. Culture which once seemed invisible, as it was habitually
> inculcated into people over time and became sedimented into well-
> worn social routines, now surfaces as a problem. Taken-for-granted
> tacit knowledge about what to do, how to respond to particular groups
> of people and what judgement of taste to make, now becomes prob-
> lematic. Within consumer culture newspapers, magazines, television
> and radio all offer advice on how to cope with a range of new situa-
> tions, risks and opportunities—yet this only adds to rather than
> reduces complexity. (Featherstone, 1995: 5; emphasis added)

Part of the task of understanding ideology is to comprehend how
people become members of society, living their lives with a certain
(or perhaps uncertain) sense of identity and seeing things from particular perspectives. This means understanding socialization. Given the
complexities of modern, or indeed postmodern society, socialization
is no longer—if it ever was—a simple, direct inculcation of social
norms, values, and behaviours. The diversity of values within multicultural or multi-ethnic societies, as well as the diversity of signs,

images, and representations that we encounter on a daily basis, means that it has become difficult to track the exact process of gaining an identity, whether the person doing the tracking is a researcher or an individual engaged in a personal quest.

Added to this diversity is what Neil Postman and Steve Powers refer to as the return to **tribalism** in American society, "as different ethnic, racial and religious groups aggressively reject the metaphor of the 'melting' pot." These groups "insist on the supremacy of their unique identities and demand that our social, political and educational systems recognize the reality of **multiculturalism**" (Postman & Powers, 1992: 157–58). In Canada this cultural diversity has been reinforced through the adopted metaphor of the cultural mosaic and supported by the federal multicultural policy introduced in 1971 and the Multicultural Act of 1988.

The emergence of the concept of identity politics has come from this recognition of diversity. Identity politics suggests that a cultural group should have ownership or control of its own formation and should be able to define its own conditions without intervention from outsiders; further, the media, government, or any other force should not simplistically define the group's identity and possibilities, especially in stereotypic ways. Cultural diversity deepens the complexity of a child's (or anyone else's) induction into a particular society and cultural milieu.

Identity Formation in Cultural Diversity

The genesis of individual identity is not only complicated by the dynamics of collective representations that attempt to dictate individual realities, but also takes place in a multiplicity of sites, including homes, schools, churches, and arts and sports facilities. This process, often described as "creating subjectivities," demands a necessary multiplicity of ideas, actions, and behaviours if individuals are to function effectively within various roles and contexts.

Socialization by its very nature is an interactive process whereby an individual is integrated, with varying degrees of success, into a particular cultural context. An important historical, as well as anthropological, question then arises: was (or is) socialization any easier or more straightforward historically (and in far-off societies) than it is today in North America? Certainly, for a newborn entering North American society now, the details of the process, as well as the very "stuff" of socialization—the material goods, the communications systems, the surroundings in general—are very complicated.

For example, how does learning the complexities of the landscape of an African savannah—the joys, dangers, and resources of that environment—differ from learning the complexities of an urban subway system? What are the roles of knowledge, language, and conceptualization in these two experiences? Imagine someone walking out onto the savannah at daybreak. From what one knows of Africa (which admittedly may be only a little and may well come largely from media representations), what does one think that person would see or do? Now, imagine someone walking into a subway early in the morning. Obviously, this individual is exposed to a different set of cultural conditions from the African situation, including well-established values and norms. Most obviously, the person is exposed to seemingly endless advertisements—and not just on the walls—amounting to a barrage of representations. The person has to engage in a commercial transaction just to use the subway system, not only paying a fare, but perhaps buying a cup of coffee, chocolate bar, or newspaper at a station kiosk. All of this activity, this everyday experience, is ideologically charged. The biggest difference between the two scenarios—African savannah and urban subway station— might be called a "consumer ideology." In supporting this ideology, particular processes of socialization—complex cultural or societal dictates or societal determinants—have gained legitimacy.

In other words, what seems different about contemporary socio-cultural reality is the ideological force and intention behind the representations in society and how these representations work. For example, everything from family values to various strategies adopted by beer company advertisements ("I am Canadian," for example) are ideologically charged. Young people feel the power of this force particularly strongly (partly because they don't have the cash to respond in the way they might like). Marketing pressure, with youth as an important consumer target, is almost extreme—the must-have shoes, designer clothes, hot new gadgets. It is not enough just to purchase these highly advertised consumer items; the current trend is for us to wear and bear company logos on our clothes and caps and jackets. Consumers are now walking billboards, which only supports the ever-growing consumer ideology. If these consumers were asked to advertise one of these items, they might expect payment for their services, yet, as it is, they seem quite comfortable doing it for nothing.

Paradoxically, by purchasing and wearing advertisement-laden clothes, we are paying the company for its advertisement and at the same time doing the advertising. The cultural baggage is getting heavier and more costly, in every sense of both of those words. Modern, complex, industrialized, consumer-based societies have such an array of goods, and different communities or subcultures place different values on them, that we seem to have infinite choices that go far beyond the "basic needs" that our imagined African savannah dweller might be working to satisfy.

The inundation of advertisements seems, in the words of Herbert Schiller (1973), to be occupying all available spaces, which only adds to the masking of, and ultimate deflection from, important socio-economic and political issues. As James Twitchell states:

> Adcult is there when we blink, it's there when we listen, it's there when we touch, it's even there to be smelled in scent strips when we open a magazine. There is barely an empty space in our culture not already carrying commercial messages. Look anywhere: in schools there is Channel One; in movies there is product placement; ads are in urinals, played on telephone hold, in alphanumeric displays in taxis, sent unannounced to fax machines, inside catalogs, on the video in front of the Stairmaster at the gym, on T-shirts, at the doctor's office, on grocery carts, on parking meters, on tees at golf holes, on inner city basketball backboards, piped in along with Muzak … ad nauseam (and yes, even on airline vomit bags). We have to shake magazines like rag dolls to free up their pages from the "blow-in" inserts and then wrestle out the stapled or glued-in ones before reading can begin. We now have to fast-forward through some five minutes of advertising that open rental videotapes. President Clinton's inaugural parade featured a

Budweiser float. At the Smithsonian, the Orkin Pest Control Company sponsored an exhibit on exactly what it advertises it kills: insects. No venue is safe. Is there a blockbuster museum show not decorated with corporate logos? Public broadcasting is littered with "underwriting announcements" which look and sound almost exactly like what PBS claims they are not: commercials. (Twitchell, 1996: 198)

At major sporting events, corporate advertisements are everywhere. Educational institutions have taken on corporate sponsorship of programs, with the proviso that they can display advertising logos on computers and soda machines. Within consumer economy, many ordinary individuals become so caught up in the whirl of consumption that they are often blinded to the social inequalities inherent in the income distribution and taxation system or the race and gender relations that surround them and have such an impact on their lives.

Identity Formation as Dialectical Process

To comprehend the complex process of socialization in contemporary society, we need to continually remind ourselves that the everyday life spaces we occupy demand a certain knowledge, language descriptors or vocabularies, and basic value positions in order for them to make sense. There is an assumption that "sense-making" is part of being human as well as part of socialization. The other side of the experience is narcosis, of various sorts. For us, narcosis describes a process of social and psychological mystification, a kind of disengagement from the social, political, and cultural happenings of a society, a sort of "dozing off." As Paul Willis puts it so well: "One of the most important general functions of ideology is the way in which it turns uncertain and fragile cultural resolutions and outcomes into a pervasive naturalism" (Willis, 1981: 102). Once something has become natural or at least appears to be natural, it often becomes impenetrable, and a critical analysis of its place in social thought and action becomes less of a possibility.

Often, in the exploration of socialization, the researcher assumes that it is a coercive process, that the neophyte or newborn or developing child or student or worker has little or no choice in the matter. Language, as well as a multitude of other fundamental aspects of social life, seems to be socially and culturally determined. Today, although choice has become something of a buzz word, in our everyday lives we seldom articulate our choices in ways that explain or underline their origins, the contexts out of which they have arisen. What is the real nature of today's consumer choices? Who has framed the accepted legitimacy of those choices?

This matter of choice can be explored in at least a couple of ways. One is the classic idea of the **tabula rasa** as suggested by John Locke (1632–1704). This assumes that the neophyte is a blank slate upon which the society and culture (the adults) write and that the process involves a passive receipt of the prescribed cultural information and messages necessary for someone to become a functioning member of society. Another approach is represented by the conceptual explorations of phenomenologists such as Edmund Husserl (1859–1938), who recognize the importance of **intentionality**, arguing that people participate in the creation of the social world themselves, through their choices, and are not simply formed by social forces, and that individuals will intend what they are aware of—that consciousness is always *consciousness of* something. This idea attributes a far greater degree of freedom to the individual than does the *tabula rasa* approach to socialization.

If we accept the perspective that within the lifelong process of socialization people are co-producers of their social reality, exhibiting intentionality and making choices, the narcosis thesis becomes less compelling or at least takes on a different meaning. A person could choose to go to sleep, accepting socio-cultural realities as they are framed. This distinction becomes fundamentally and profoundly important when we recognize the impact of ideology upon the individual, recognizing that we tend to make choices within an array of ideological representations.

Socialization Theory

The symbolic interactionists Charles Horton Cooley, George Herbert Mead, and Herbert Blumer provide a powerful analysis of socialization. They believe that the individual entering society is activated by the social environment and has an active co-producer role within it. As Cooley suggests, "The self and society are twin born" (Cooley, 1962: 5). He uses the metaphor of the looking glass to demonstrate how others influence the way we see ourselves. Just as we look into the mirror to see a reflection of our physical being, we see ourselves through the reactions of others, and their opinions help to determine who we are. In other words, how we think of ourselves is formulated around our perception of how others judge us. This co-produced, negotiated reality recognizes the individual not as a passive participant overwhelmed by the coercive power of the surrounding environment but as an active participant. In doing so it establishes a dialectical, two-way relationship, which is contrary to the "fill 'er up" approach wherein the individual is shaped and produced by the society in a deterministic manner. The child enters a society and culture that is already underway, that is ongoing and, that, at least tacitly, is understood by those who live in it. The **significant others** to the child (parents, guardians, family, friends, and other caregivers) have tremendous impact upon him or her.

In George Herbert Mead's (1934) term, **taking the role of the other** means seeing the world through the eyes and experiences of one's significant others, internalizing the understandings of those with whom we communicate most immediately. At the early stages of development children have no self-history or experience for dealing with novel situations. They are vulnerable, therefore, to the attitudes of significant others who give definition to experience; indeed, children experience themselves indirectly, through the eyes of others. Mead writes about this at two levels: first, the experiential, which comes in relationship to immediate significant others, followed by the abstract relationship to the **generalized other**, which represents the values and commitments of the wider social community. In terms of identity politics, the created subjectivity of the individual, as shaped and created within a social context, is filled with diverse images, values, and choices. In itself, the process is much more like the development over a long period of time of an old-growth forest rather than the replanting of a tree farm or plantation: our identities have become studies in "biodiversity." We live a multiplicity of roles within a multiplicity of contexts, rather than as persons with a monoculture, a singularity or uniformity of identity. The complexity of this forest metaphor is significant. As we recognize the postmodernist multiplicity of identities, we also need to recognize the "McDonaldization of society" as explored by George Ritzer (1993; see also Shiva, 1997). We live in a time in which the contradiction between cultural diversity and monoculturalism seems clear.

The diversity of experience, image, representation, and reality confronting the neophyte's search for identity demands both choice (recognizing the class, gender, and ethnic limitations that surround such a term) and cultural knowledge about what choice is legitimate within the competing dynamics of the complex socio-cultural environment. This matter of legitimate choice, or even legitimacy, raises a number of questions. Is there a social consensus? If so, what is it? In terms of the classical Durkheimian paradigm, what is it that provides or sustains social solidarity? What is the glue that binds individuals to the social norms and, in a wider sense, the normative structures that make up society's wider value system or consensus? Is there some semblance of a Durkheimian "conscience collective"? If so, who is advantaged or disadvantaged by this? Although the process of socialization may be seen as dialectical within Mead's theoretical perspective, we need to remind ourselves of the diverse complexity of the socio-cultural choices facing people today. As we integrate ourselves into our society, creating our identities within our families and communities, we live within a globalized milieu that is shaped and constructed by forces well beyond the explicit powers of our own communities.

The Ideological Impact of Socialization

The dilemmas of contemporary experience, then, are determined not only by the contents of socio-cultural normative structures, but also by the processes of acquisition related to such socio-cultural moments of entry into the social world. If we begin to look beyond the impact of our "significant others" to the role of socializing agents such as the media —through movies, TV situation comedies, dramas, documentaries, news, editorials, advertisements on T-shirts and baseball caps, and so on— the dynamic facing a child's development in society today is truly complex.

Although researchers have not yet established the existence of a direct impact of the media on individuals, many social scientists do agree that how the media select and shape certain issues for presentation does have a major influence on how people see and experience things. Through the process of representation, different types of media have successfully conditioned various audiences into an accommodation with prepackaged messages. Ideological presentations and representations can, and do, mystify social reality and cloud or distort social perceptions. As Graham Knight states: "The press may not be successful much of the time in telling people what to think, but it is stunningly successful in telling its readers what to think about" (Knight, 2001: 108, quoting Cohen, 1963: 13). As this social conditioning to certain ideas becomes internalized, it is usually expressed through the taken-for-granted ideological practices of everyday life. In exploring the unconscious nature of ideology, John Fiske points out:

> Ideology is therefore a process that seeks pacifically to transform a particular distribution of powers, choices and directions into appearing "natural," "fair," and "normal"; into appearing as simply the expression of a shared "commonsense": the "only" or "best thing to do" in the circumstances. It is the successful installation of this common frame of reference in the institutions and experiences of daily life—at home, on television, in the press, in the curriculum and the culture of the school, at work, in political parties, religious organizations and trade unions—that the Italian Marxist Antonio Gramsci called "hegemony." Under hegemony, ideology is not directly imposed but continually composed through a mobile strategy of shifting alliances and compromises formed in pursuit of a government by "consensus." (Fiske, 1986: 210–11)

Ideology, then, is not something imposed from "above," but something that continually impacts on our everyday lives, in and through each of us. It feeds the daily substance of life in which we cohere, recognize our selves, and move and act as unified subjects.

To suggest that society is a "set of forces" (Hale, 1995) acting upon the individual is one thing. To recognize the differential power sites that form sets of forces acting on, influencing, conditioning, and programming the validated cultural blueprint (some might prefer the term "software") is something else—something much more complex. Christine Gledhill illustrates this complexity:

> For feminists, as for Marxists, the media have figured as a major instrument of *ideological domination*. The problem with this notion ... is that it makes it difficult to conceptualize a position from which to resist or challenge it, except through the values or ideas of the dominant elite which necessarily exclude the mystified masses. A way of moving beyond this impasse was offered in the thinking of the Italian Marxist, Antonio Gramsci ... which permitted a decisive reformulation of the concept of ideology, displacing the notion of domination by that of *hegemony*. According to Gramsci, since power in a bourgeois democracy is as much a matter of persuasion and consent as of force, it is never secured once and for all.
>
> Any dominant group has to a greater or lesser degree to acknowledge the existence of those whom it dominates by winning the consent of competing or marginalized groups in society. Unlike the fixed grip over society implied by the "domination," "hegemony" is won in the to-and-fro of *negotiation* between competing social, political and ideological forces through which power is contested, shifted or reformed. *Representation* is a key site in such struggle, since the power of definition is a major source of hegemony. ... Thus in the process of negotiating hegemony, ideologies may shift their ground, the central consensus may be changed, and "the real" reconstructed. (Gledhill, 1997: 348; emphasis in original)

The process of negotiating hegemony becomes even more difficult when we factor in the modern educational experience with its school curricula that generally lack a critical consciousness approach. The possibility of gaining a critical awareness of the tacit or taken-for-granted aspects of a socio-cultural milieu becomes less likely, given these circumstances. This situation could be equated to asking a baby to become a rock climber. The lack of an approach that includes development of a critical consciousness is commonplace, and these days it is linked to the growing **corporatization** of the public educational system. Emphasizing this point, Henry Giroux states:

> The corporatizing of public education has taken a distinct turn as we approach the twenty-first century. No longer content merely to argue for the application of business principles to the organization of school-ing, the forces of corporate culture have adopted a much more radical agenda. Central to this agenda is the attempt to transform public educa-tion from a public good, benefiting all students, to a private good designed to expand the profits of investors, educate students as consumers, and train young people for the low-paying jobs of the new global market-place. (Giroux, 2000: 85)

The focus on the preparation of workers for the new global market-place creates a situation in which certain bodies of knowledge are in high demand while others are ignored. As Donaldo Macedo points out in his Foreward to Paulo Freire's classic study *Pedagogy of Freedom*, there is a "selection process" at work "that prioritizes certain bodies of knowledge while discouraging or suffocating other discourses." This process of selec-tion, he says, "is linked to something beyond education: ideology."

> Thus, the curriculum selection and organization that favor a disartic-ulated technical training over courses in critical theory, which would enable students to make linkages with other bodies of knowledge so as to gain a more comprehensive understanding of reality, points to the very ideology that attempts to deny its existence through a false claim of neutrality. The insidious nature of ideology is its ability to make itself invisible. (Macedo, 1998: xiii).

Fundamental to the process of socialization is the internalization of vari-ous components of the social environment, such as values, norms, mores, behaviours and attitudes, artistic taste, and basic understandings of how institutions work. The arrangement establishes a kind of "expected" symmetry of meaning between the individual and the surrounding social world. The notion of symmetry becomes increasingly problematic as varieties of identities or multiple identities become the norm. Mike Featherstone, for example, suggests that people may find a transient consensus, what he terms "fragile consensus," in which aesthetic communities may be established for short periods of time. He gives the examples of rock festivals organized as "Feed the World" and "Band-Aid" benefit concerts (Featherstone, 1995: 47).

This period of establishing a sense of identity or personality, while still a profound experience within an individual's early life, is increasingly seen as a time for building possible multiple identities as the dynamics of culture and society become less homogeneous or singular in nature. There is a nostalgic leap and moment that penetrates all of this—the desire, the wish, for a unified, simplistic identity, unhindered by a fragmented social world filled with complexity and multiplicity. And, to a large extent, the idea of such a unified personality or identity, based on a common value system, still holds within the experience of socialization that characterizes most people's everyday life.

At the level of secondary socialization, the induction into institutionalized subworlds, this unified conceptualization still holds as well. The commitment to cleanliness obsessively proffered by the McDonald's fast food chain, for example, is generally uncontested. Indeed, from a new employee's point of view, if violated, the ideal of cleanliness could be the cause for being fired. Classic renderings of this socialization process, such as Peter Berger's and Thomas Luckmann's *The Social Construction of Reality* (1967), utilize such phrases as *"the* world" or the "world *tout court"*— meaning that an envelop encloses us, almost like a company's uniform encloses its worker. These authors note that part of the role of socializing institutions is to overcome the artificial nature of the new realities they represent by attempting to bring home meaning to the individual: "These manoeuvres are necessary because an internalized reality is already there, persistently 'in the way' of new internalizations" (Berger & Luckmann, 1967: 143). A glance at media representation of the multicultural, multiethnic realities in our communities indicates the intense complexity of what "bringing home" might mean.

Social Construction: Reification and Plausibility in Society

The **social constructivist** position, articulated in its early renderings by theorists such as Berger and Luckmann, recognizes the dialectical nature of socialization as well as the significantly dialectical nature of constructing social worlds. As they put it, "*Society is a human product. Society is an objective reality. Humans are a social product*" (Berger & Luckmann, 1967: 61; emphasis in original). In other words, not only do human beings construct and produce a social world, but they are also shaped and produced by what they and others have built. To suggest that children may be a product of a specific socio-cultural, historical period is not to be overly deterministic but to be alert to the profound dynamics of contemporary society. To be a co-producer is to transcend the victim posture. To be critically alert demands understanding and recognition of the impact of many objective forces, structures, and symbolic systems on the individual. To follow our metaphor, it is to be awake.

However, as the objective social realities become solidified or sedimented within societies, they also become reified. The concept of **reification** is most easily understood as the "apprehension of human phenomena as if they were things" (Berger & Luckmann 1967: 89). Essentially, the process involves forgetting the human origins of phenomena, a conceptualization that avoids or is inattentive to the human participation in world construction. For example, the Nike "swoosh" (i.e., the check mark symbol) not only is of human origin, but also predates Nike by some time. Most of us encountered a form of the symbol now known as the swoosh as a check mark on our early school projects to indicate that we have done well. As a contemporary symbolic presentation, with a huge advertising and media impact, it is the product of human consciousness.

The example of the Nike swoosh takes us once again to the profound impact of the process of internalization in contemporary society—a fundamental dynamic of socialization. As Peter Berger points out, "Internalization is rather the re-absorption into consciousness of the objectivated world in such a way that the structures of this world come to determine the subjective structures of consciousness itself" (Berger, 1967: 15).

Featherstone argues that this pervasive mix of economic realities and cultural realities is in need of profoundly new interpretations within postmodernism. For example, he suggests that "the analysis of consumption has been largely neglected in favour of production and distribution" (Featherstone, 1995: 17). Of interest here—again with regard to our Nike example—is that in addition to the classic notions of **use value** and **exchange value** put forward by Marx, under the conditions of contemporary capitalist society we must also recognize the idea of **sign value**. Commodities and their advertised expressions have cultural implications more far-reaching than we often comprehend or imagine. Indeed, Featherstone argues that these signs serve as markers within the cultural and status domains of society. In general, he notes, we must reckon with the **carriers of culture**; indeed, we must explore the place of cultural producers within the cultural industries, which create, sustain, and fragment social realities. We must not only find new ground in our social realities, but also reckon with profoundly new perspectives for attempting to comprehend these modern or postmodern realities.

> These are not only the new forms of art and intellectual life, but also the piling-up of forms with which to interpret this process, some of which are *pedagogies to help the uninitiated learn how* to decontrol their emotions, to play with a variety of new and potentially threatening images and sensations without the fear of a total loss of control must also be considered. (Featherstone 1995: 50; emphasis added)

The search for identity—the structuring and restructuring of personal identity—does not, in modern terms, allow for or confirm a singular conceptualization. The fragmentation of signs, images, and values within postmodernist culture demands a new and more agile comprehension of socialization and of the layering of its ideological dynamics.

Perhaps one of the most taken-for-granted aspects of society at any time in history (but particularly now) is the precarious nature of society itself. All sorts of structural, interactional elements within societies are set in place to give legitimacy and plausibility to everything that is taken-for-granted as well as everything that is problematic; ideologies have a particular role in this phenomenon. As Berger puts it, "Let the institutional order be so interpreted as to hide, as much as possible, its *constructed* character" (Berger, 1967: 33). In a person's life, when, if ever, does this constructed character become revealed, articulated, and analyzed? When do people begin to examine what is being hidden, and how, why, where, and when? Or, who is hiding it and for what purposes and ends? Surely, an authentic understanding of democratic life hinges on the answer to these questions—or at least on the attempt to answer them.

The question of plausibility is dynamically intertwined with the legitimacy of particular views, norms, or values that come into contact with or confront one another. As Berger notes in his analysis of religion (1967), plausibility structures become most evident and precarious in cases of **acculturation**—the adapting to, or adopting of, a different culture. Not only do the various elements of each culture become most evident, but they can also become highly contested, problematic, and, indeed, no longer always plausible. The same thing can happen whenever contradictory forces of "expertise" on one side and "democratization of knowledge" on the other collide or, indeed, take hold in such critical fields as health care, education, and politics. In the case of the legitimacy and plausibility of Western medicine, for instance, people now take time to search the Internet for information on medical diagnoses and treatments; physicians, aware of this Internet information-blitz, may respond to their patients with admiration for what they call "improved patient-directed interest in their own health" (CBC *Broadcast 1*, 5 January 1998). But to suggest that someone has legitimate control of such domains of human knowledge and interaction under contemporary circumstances is naive. Indeed, the diversity of possibilities for health is not only "awesome," but also astounding—at times, frightening. What seems to be plausible—or is plausible—today often overwhelms us.

Combining the metaphorical power of health and culture, and the contradictions that surface, John Ralston Saul, in *Reflections of a Siamese Twin: Canada at the End of the Twentieth Century* writes:

> In a way this was the real question raised by Jacques Godbout in *Les Têtes à Papineau*. Together his Siamese-twin heroes are complex,

interesting, contradictory, original. Separate them and they become like everyone else. Normalcy has its attractions. Its comforts. "It's for your own good?" said the doctor. "One can't spend one's life half this and half that. ... Gentlemen, you are nothing more than half-men?" Of course, with normalcy you lose the disadvantages of McLuhan's "discontinuity." You also lose its advantages. You join the majority school of the monolithic nation-state, providing your geographic reality permits it. The one question Godbout didn't raise was the rate of mortality in operations to separate Siamese twins. It is very rare for both to live. Sometimes one survives. Usually neither." (Saul, 1997: 116)

What of the difficult ground that has to be traversed by every parent, teacher, and person as they participate in the socialization of youth in society? As Neil Postman argues, television is really the "first curriculum" (see Postman, 1979, 1982), no matter how much educators might like to think otherwise. To what are children exposed these days? To what are they socialized? What processes and images enclose this experience of socialization? Indeed, of these processes and images, what is internalized? Again, is there a recognized consensus around what we would call our "society" or even a "dominant culture"? Does there need to be some reciprocity of communication to keep diversity afloat within a multicultural society? What place do the material/technical realities, the cultural toys or artefacts of the society (for example, the automobile, television, computer), play in our reconciliation of all these themes?

In the following chapters we will explore how power and advantage are expressed amid the complexities of contemporary society. Obviously, we are socialized into understandings of power and advantage in a way similar to the ways in which we are socialized into so many other of our lives' understandings. Since ideologies play a role in politicizing public and private spaces, the politics of race/ethnicity *in public/private spaces* is central in a multicultural, multi-ethnic society. The constant, continuing representations and distortions advantage and/or disadvantage individuals and groups, and the sites of advantage and disadvantage— the sites of social inequality—are most commonly manifested within the domains of social class, gender, race, and ethnicity, which have both public and personal sites of expression. To be critically alert to representations and reifications is, then, an act of critical consciousness within the struggles of everyday life.

CHAPTER 4

Politicizing, Depoliticizing, and the Creation of Advantage

Yearning is the word that best describes a common psychological state shared by many of us, cutting across boundaries of race, class, gender, and sexual practice. Specifically, in relation to the post modernist deconstruction of "master" narratives, the yearning that wells in the hearts and minds of those whom such narratives have silenced is the longing for critical voice.... It never surprises me when black folks respond to the critique of **essentialism**, especially when it denies the validity of identity politics by saying, "Yeah, it's easy to give up identity, when you got one." Should we not be suspicious of postmodern critiques of the "subject" when they surface at a historical moment when many subjugated people feel themselves coming to voice for the first time. Though an apt and oftentimes appropriate comeback, it does not really intervene in the discourse in a way that alters and transforms. (hooks, 1990: 27–28)

L ike the concepts of ideology and socialization, a political formation like identity politics, as bell hooks suggests (though it is more of a challenge than a suggestion), has to be placed within a larger, wider frame—within the contexts of people's everyday lives. Ideologies work to **politicize** and **depoliticize** our social, economic, and political environments; thus, the "yearning that wells in the hearts and minds," the "silencing," and the "longing for the critical voice."

But in this case, too, the idea of politics, or of what is deemed political, has to be understood in a very different way than usual. It has to range far beyond the standard meaning of ballot-box politics or of people working on our behalf in a legislature or government. What we consider to be political turns on a wider understanding of power, particularly of power as a political dynamic. Max Weber, for instance, theorized power as a matter of "power over," which can be counterpointed by Michel Foucault's understanding that "power is everywhere—it is circulating." To see politics as a ubiquitous phenomenon extends both our perceptions and our possibilities for acting, thinking, and living within our communities.

Our point of departure, therefore, is the politics of everyday experience, the embedded power relationships of everyday life, ranging from children's experiences of power dynamics in classrooms to workplace grievances and the structured discriminatory practices that give one gender a constant advantage over the other. These moments become one of the most important sites of ideological expression and formation, and they are often transformed into the projects of extraparliamentary politics or the political activism of social movements. This is not to suggest that legislated actions or the politics of the ballot box do not also work at the ideological level. In most cases, the political jurisdiction legislating particular laws constructs these laws out of and within the ideological formations legitimated within the politics of our communities and neighbourhoods. The ideological backdrops for our laws are the everyday structural arrangements and practices in which the ideological formations make sense and become established.

As we have seen in our various definitions of ideology (Chapter 2), ideologies are not always necessarily what is ordinarily called political. First, an ideology can be a self-interested, partial truth constructed to serve the advantage of a particular group in society; for example, "the business of business is to make a profit." Second, an ideology can be seen as a socially contextualized formation of knowledge—that is, all knowledge is ideological—that emerges out of a specific social interest or context, such as science or religion. Third, there is the more obviously political definition: ideologies are socially constructed systems of ideas, which means that they take on symbolic status and meaning within societies. As a result, they become indexes for action or the organization of various social and political structures, such as fascism, liberalism, and conservatism, as well as socialism and **feminism**.

In essence, however, the first and the second definitions are just as political as the third, in the wider sense of the term: they create and represent systems of power; the power they manifest relates to social and economic conditions and structures. "The business of business is to make profit" puts other priorities in their place, which is below profit and often out of sight. In addition, because ideologies are embedded in everyday life through both conscious and subconscious means, they exert an extraordinary power—and power is above everything else always a political condition or determinant.

The Structuring of Advantage

For the most part, we tend to experience the power relationships of everyday life—relationships embedded in the encounters we have with others and the structural dynamics of our social existence—as personal or private moments. Indeed, these relationships are often masked or hidden in a way that seems to make them only personal or private. Therefore, to politicize an aspect of everyday life is to bring it before the public, before the collective society.

For example, to marry is a public act, a chosen representation of an aspect of life that is legitimated in the public realm; marriage is an institution given power by the public, by the government or government officials. To co-habit can be public as well, but it is not equally public in legitimacy (yet) or indeed in forms of representation. Therefore, to move from the public moment to the politicized public moment is an identifiable step. The personal becomes the public.

In essence, too, the moment that politicized power enters the public domain is the moment when the creation of advantage and disadvantage becomes more apparent. Contemporary life is filled with numerous politicized human personal and public debates. In part, this process, if viewed methodologically, is a public exposition of the ideological positions that determine or govern the affairs of everyday life. To politicize is to make explicit the power relations embedded in the lived experience of people's daily lives (see Bailey, 1986). The great outcry and debate regarding **political correctness** (see Richer & Weir, 1995) essentially represent a public moaning regarding what was previously determined as sacred ground; that is, "Don't explode my ideological position, and please don't expose it!" To politicize is to engage the status quo, to question what is taken for granted, to declassify that which has been kept hidden by the government, the professions, and the corporations.

To depoliticize has a contrary, but equally political, effect upon society and the ideological structures embedded in its power relations. (Of course, there is also the process of repoliticizing, that is, once again returning something to the public domain. Repoliticizing quite simply recognizes the on-going dynamic of the politics of everyday life and experience.) The dynamics of depoliticization can involve several acts:

1. taking the political flavour out of some issue or dispute;
2. (re)moving a public dispute to the private domain;
3. disengaging from political discourse;
4. removing an issue or dispute from a publicly contested domain;
5. not revealing underlying viewpoints or interests;
6. removing from recognition certain advantages to certain groups; and
7. using euphemisms as forms of diversion.

The process of depoliticization in contemporary society is filled with intricate ideological moments. For example, within the ideology of individualism one is assumed responsible for one's own economic failure or success. If there is unemployment in a time of economic crisis, "blaming the victim" reveals a failure to recognize the problem as structural, thus freeing the state of its responsibility. On December 10, 1996 Canadian Prime Minister Jean Chrétien made a remark pertinent to this point at a CBC Town Hall meeting: "If your specialty does not lead to give you a job in Saskatoon, perhaps you can go to Regina or elsewhere. But I'm not living there" (CBC, 1996), thus revealing a fundamental lack of knowledge of the reality of structural unemployment.

Another example of depoliticization is the process of **medicalization**, the professional appropriation of domains that were once natural or normal human experiences, such as childbirth and menopause (see

Bolaria, 1995: 214; Bailey & Gayle, 1993: 438). As Janet Stoppard notes:

> The medical view of women's bodies implicitly takes male biology as the norm for human health. Against this male-biased standard, female reproductive biology, with its inherent cyclicity, is seen as deviant. Women's biological differences from men are recast in terms of illness or disease. In effect, the medical model reproduces women as deficient or dysfunctional men. (Stoppard, 1992: 126)

On another level, to medicalize alcoholism is to put it under the control of the professional medical community—to make it above all else a medical problem, setting it apart from the social, structural problems out of which it may have emerged, such as unemployment, inadequate housing, poverty, and work-related stress.

To depoliticize is to hide or obscure the structural nature of a social issue—to take it out of the public debate or discourse. Today's personal and public experience and discourse tend to be governed or determined by processes that engage or disengage various debates. To be capable of recognizing these processes is to overcome the most narcotic dimensions of contemporary society. A further, necessary step is to participate in social action directed at solving the problems. As Paulo Freire states, "Only beings who can reflect upon the fact that they are determined are capable of freeing themselves" (Freire, 1970: 28). That reflection, though, is itself driven by ideology—by the ideological formations that are accessible to the particular individual. Just to begin developing a critical consciousness demands alertness, method, and imagination.

Building a Critical Perspective, Resisting the Constructed Advantage: Freire, Chomsky, and hooks

In her book *Teaching to Transgress*, bell hooks outlines her own starting point for developing a critical consciousness. She came to theory, she says, when she was still a child: "I came to theory because I was hurting—the pain within me was so intense that I could not go on living. I came to theory desperate, wanting to comprehend—to grasp what was happening around and within me. Most importantly, I wanted to make the hurt go away. I saw in theory then a location for healing" (hooks, 1994: 59).

Another critical theorist, Terry Eagleton, also comments on the power of the child's perspective:

> Children make the best theorists, since they have not yet been educated into accepting our routine social practices as "natural," and so insist on posing to those practices the most embarrassingly general and fundamental questions, regarding them with a wondering estrangement which we adults have long forgotten. Since they do not yet grasp our social practices as inevitable, they do not see why we might not do things differently. (Quoted in hooks, 1994: 59)

Significantly for us, Eagleton makes, once again, the link between ideology and socialization.

hooks and two other contemporary thinkers, Paulo Freire and Noam Chomsky, share a demand for the unity of theory and action—the nexus of thought, word, and action called praxis. All demand the democratization of knowledge and information, the recognition of the distinction between the passive receipt of knowledge and the active generation of knowledge. If human life is to be liberatory, actions need to be democratically formed and based both in reflective theorizing and the generation of knowledge. As Noam Chomsky puts it, "There is, in my opinion, much too little inquiry into these matters. My personal feeling is that citizens of the democratic societies should undertake a course of intellectual self-defense to protect themselves from manipulation and control, and to lay the basis for more meaningful democracy" (Chomsky, 1989: viii).

To be a critical participant is to recognize the power of ideological formations to shape, influence, and create inequalities and differential structures of advantage. Neil Postman calls this task, as applied to educational institutions, "crap-detecting" (Postman & Weingartner, 1969: 1). Edward Said puts it another way, suggesting that people should always deploy a certain scepticism as part of their "intellectual and critical faculty" (Said, 1994: 140). People should refuse to become sponges, merely absorbing prepackaged information. Television messages, in particular, represent a thoroughly processed ideological package.

Paulo Freire

Paulo Freire, the Brazilian educational theorist best known for his book *Pedagogy of the Oppressed*, describes this process as conscientization: "the process in which men not as recipients, but as knowing subjects, achieve a deepening awareness of both the socio-cultural reality which shapes their lives and of their capacity to transform that reality" (Freire, 1970: 27). He adds: "Only beings who can reflect upon the fact that they are determined are capable of freeing themselves. Their reflectiveness results not just in a vague and uncommitted awareness, but in the exercise of a profoundly transforming action upon the determining reality" (Freire, 1970: 28).

Freire's work emphasizes the importance of moving from a defined methodology of problem-solving to the more critical moment of problematizing or calling something into question. To problem-solve is to use a well-defined method to bring a question or puzzle to a conclusion or answer: $x + y = z$. Given the value of x (2) and the value of y (4), we can determine the value of z (6). This kind of logic, this way of knowing, means that the results are contained within a certain frame, even though an authentic question may well be one for which we (teacher and student) really may not know the answer. The methodology of problematizing demands that we gain a distance from the object of study to see it in new ways. At the same time, we have to be careful not to gain so much distance that we lose sight of the everyday experience involved in the question or invalidate the answer through abstraction.

For example, to begin to question or fundamentally gain distance from the issue of the automobile as a dominant form of transportation is not only to recognize it as a technology that pollutes the atmosphere and causes severe environmental problems, but also to recognize the political nature of driving a car and an understanding of possible action around the issue (Illich, 1974; Alvord, 2000). This process is not neutral. The automobile is not simply an object of technical elegance to be used as a convenient mode of transportation or as an *objet d'art*. In the period after World War II, "the automobile became the keystone of the North American economy," as writer Alexander Wilson points out. The changes "didn't happen by themselves," he notes: "Several US corporations, most notably General Motors, practised ruthless marketing strategies that would ultimately ensure the car its central place in North American culture." Furthermore, the automobile has had an enormous impact not just on urbanization but also on the landscape in general—dividing "the landscape, and our experience of it, into discrete zones" (Wilson, 1991: 28–29). The automobile has come to exert a powerful control over everyday life from our relationship to food and work to community development.

Freire politicizes the nature of our experience of objects. He also examines and politicizes our understanding of words, of language. If individuals in a society don't see the political power embedded in the words, thoughts, and actions of their everyday lives, they soon become consumed by a passive, almost inert, relationship with the dynamics of power. Words become masks, hiding social/economic/cultural realities, rather than potent elements in critical analysis.

Within the rigour of this process of critical knowing, Freire also demands a reconstruction; he demands that we transform our understanding and, indeed, transform ourselves. We begin to see the categories of thought and the words that shape our existence—to see the eyes through which we see, to use E.F. Schumacher's phrase: "…you can see what is outside you, but cannot easily see that with which you see, the eye itself. And even when one has become aware of them [those categories of thought and words] it is often impossible to judge them on the basis of ordinary experience" (Schumacher, 1973: 83). Freire calls for movement from the "surface structure" (the original "codification": "the imaging, or the image itself) to the "deep structural" moment of analysis (the "decodification": "a process of description and interpretation whether of printed words, pictures…") in order to see the structural relationships that underlie social conditions (Freire, 1970: 14). With regard to illiteracy or conceptual illiteracy (the "dumbing down" process of much modern schooling), Freire writes: "Prevented from having a 'structural perception' of the facts involving them, they do not know that they cannot 'have a voice,' i.e. that they cannot exercise the right to participate consciously in the socio-historical transformation of their society, because their work does not belong to them" (Freire, 1970: 13). Freire's culture of silence, the silencing of people's voices, is a world-wide phenomenon, happening frequently through the use of force and perhaps more commonly or insidiously through the ideological masking of social relationships.

Noam Chomsky

Like Freire, Noam Chomsky also calls for a questioning of the structures of advantage in society. He recognizes the insidious mechanisms at work within governments, corporations, and the media through thought control or the shaping of citizens' perceptions of society. These necessary illusions, the manufacturing of consent (see Herman & Chomsky, 1988), led Chomsky, along with Edward Herman, to propose the propaganda model, which systematically lays out the dynamics of the media's propaganda role. Indeed, their intensive research explores the impact of the manipulation of information on people's lives and the great tragedies of human life that result.

According to Herman and Chomsky, the media's propaganda role, particularly in the area of news reporting, relies heavily on the practice of framing information. To frame news or issues is to place the material within certain boundaries in a way that achieves a calculated effect. As Chomsky suggests, "The media serve the interests of state and corporate power which are closely interlinked, framing their reporting and analysis in a manner supportive of established privilege and limiting debate and discussion accordingly" (Chomsky: 1989: 10). Framing also includes the construction of news, including its selection (the decision about what constitutes a newsworthy item), the type and quantity of research, if any, and the emphasis (or de-emphasis) granted particular news items or aspects of an issue.

The Propaganda Model

Herman and Chomsky (1988) have used the propaganda model to expose how the American government and others with money and power manipulate information in getting their messages across. As Herbert Schiller states: "For manipulation to be most effective, evidence of its presence should be non-existent. When the manipulated believe things are the way they are naturally and inevitably, manipulation is successful. In short, manipulation requires a false reality that is a continuous denial of its existence" (Schiller, 1973: 11). This collective denial of manipulation informs Herman and Chomsky's propaganda model. They identify five filters through which the raw material of news must pass, "leaving only the condensed residue fit to print":

> (1) The size, concentrated ownership, owner wealth, and profit orientation of the dominant mass-media firms; (2) advertising as the primary income source of the mass media; (3) the reliance of the media on information provided by the government, business, and "experts" funded and approved by these primary sources and agents of power; (4) "flak" as a means of disciplining the media; and (5) "anti-communism" as a national religion and control mechanism. (Herman & Chomsky, 1988: 2)

In the years since Herman and Chomsky introduced this propaganda model, media power, the essence of the first filter, has become more concentrated, with mergers, acquisitions, and, as Richard Cohen describes it, "run-amok corporate cannibalism terrorizing most of American business." He goes on to say that in the Darwinian "food chain of capitalism," small companies are "eaten by bigger companies and devoured by even more mammoth corporate interests" (Cohen, 1997: 39). In recent mergers, too, a new and more dangerous pattern of control has appeared. The most amazing example of this is the combination of Turner, a cable news company and home entertainment giant, with Time-Warner, thus joining together book and magazine publishers, record, film, and television companies, professional sports, and other cable networks—and, as if that wasn't enough, eventually adding America Online, the Internet provider (see Brym, 2001: 94). This heavy-duty corporate mixture, according to Todd Gitlin, goes by the "gaudy name of 'synergy,'" and he expresses part of how it works: "*Time*, after all, devoted a cover story to Scott Turow, a Warner Books author, timed to the Warner Bros. release of the movie *Presumed Innocent. Time* found Turow more newsworthy than *Newsweek*.

Time also featured a cover story on tornadoes the week that Warner opened its blockbuster *Twister*" (Gitlin, 1997: 9). This kind of massive but concentrated corporate culture has dominated the media agenda, controlling opinion and marginalizing dissenting voices. In the global marketplace, where commodity consumption is the highest priority, "[c]ulture and commodity become indistinguishable," as Henry Giroux points out, "and social identities are shaped almost exclusively within the ideology of consumerism" (Giroux, 2000: 67). Thus, the second filter, advertising, that indispensable element in coercion, has become the primary source of revenue for the mass media, and large advertising agencies exert a great deal of influence on the media agenda.

> The power of advertisers over television programming stems from the simple fact that they buy and pay for the programs—they are the "patrons" who provide the media subsidy. As such, the media compete for their patronage, developing specialized staff to solicit advertisers and necessarily having to explain how their programs serve advertisers' needs. The choices of these patrons greatly affect the welfare of the media, and the patrons become what William Evan calls "normative reference organizations," whose requirements and demands the media must accommodate if they are to succeed. (Herman & Chomsky, 1988: 16)

Today, advertising dominates media space to the extent that many television programs and articles in newspapers and magazines more or less play the filler role that advertisements or commercials themselves played a few decades ago (see Williams, 1974: 69). Advertisers make every effort to avoid involvement with programs containing controversial issues, sometimes refusing to buy, or even going so far as withdrawing their sponsorship, for advertising time in programs that present critical points of view. As Michael Parenti explains: "When NBC ran a documentary on the terrible conditions endured by migrant workers, citing the abuses perpetrated by Coca-Cola Food Co., Coca-Cola sharply denounced the show, and the network was unable to find a single corporate sponsor for the program" (Parenti, 1993: 36). To accentuate this point, Herman and Chomsky state: "Large corporate advertisers on television will rarely sponsor programs that engage in serious criticisms of corporate activities, such as the problem of environmental degradation, the workings of the military-industrial complex, or corporate support of and benefits from Third World tyrannies" (Herman & Chomsky, 1988: 17).

The propaganda model's third filter—the media's reliance on information provided by the government, business, and "experts"—provides a sense of authority. The sources used, Herman and Chomsky argue, "have the great merit of being recognizable and credible by their status and prestige" (Herman & Chomsky, 1988: 19). The same credibility also leaves the impression that the journalists involved are objective, which in turn leads the public to believe in the stories told and to respect the opinions given. Because journalists seldom deviate from the information thus provided, they also leave themselves less open to criticism and, especially, to charges of libel.

In the propaganda model, any criticism that the media have to absorb is referred to as "flak" (the fourth filter), which is, ostensibly, a means of disciplining the media. Flak sometimes comes from within the media itself. Richard Cohen, a former senior producer of the *CBS Evening News*, notes:

> My demise at CBS News came after Dan Rather's celebrated interview with then Vice President George Bush on the facts about the Iran-Contra escapade. What had Bush known? The interview disintegrated into a shouting match between Rather and the Vice President, who claimed we had misled him about the subject of the interview.
>
> We hadn't. I set up and choreographed the video battle. Whatever one thought about Bush or what we did, CBS., Inc. was furious with us. Station managers were complaining loudly to the network. They said we had made viewers angry at CBS, and they feared TV watchers would tune CBS out. That would be death by the dial.
>
> The Corporation didn't care about the journalism involved. They only cared that station managers and, ostensibly, viewers were not happy. Vice President Bush had been lying when he claimed to be "out of the loop" on Iran-Contra. But the televised confrontation was simply bad for business. CBS News was kind enough to allow me to leave by the door. (Cohen, 1997: 43–44)

Herman and Chomsky's final filter—anti-communism as a national religion and control mechanism—has been largely supplanted by other forces, most recently anti-terrorism, though it is still a matter of "good versus evil." This filter determines how Americans see themselves in relation to the rest of the world. It is used as a method to marshal the support of the population against an enemy, real or imagined. When news runs through this filter, it tends to leave a deposit of one person or one country as the source of all evil.

Despite the fall of the "evil" Soviet Empire, the dominant anti-communist position continues to inform the foreign policy of recent and current American administrations, both Democratic and Republican. Much the same rhetoric has come into play over wars in Indo-China or political battles in El Salvador or Nicaragua. With the 1991 Gulf War, the Iraqi president, Saddam Hussein, was made into the new enemy by means of an outright media campaign of demonization, which continues into the present with the possibility of yet another war with Iraq. In the "War on Terrorism," the single focus shifted to Osama bin Laden, leader of the terrorist network, Al-Qaeda. Cuba, located only 145 kilometres from American shores, continues to be a reminder of the threat of communism, which justifies the continuation of a 40-year trade embargo.

Douglas Rushkoff notes:

> In order to generate public support for an illogical policy, leaders need to name and demonize an enemy, then whip up an emotional fury against the demon. Anyone remaining against the proposed policy needs to be minimized, sidelined or marginalized. This way people who oppose the public relations objectives are made to feel absolutely alone. (Rushkoff, 1996: 24)

As mentioned earlier, President George W. Bush put it in stark, simplistic terms before the start of the war in Afghanistan: "Either you are with us, or you are with the terrorists"(Bush, 2001).

Herman and Chomsky (1988) suggest that the elements of the propaganda model are not mutually exclusive; they interact with and reinforce each other in the process of information manipulation. The forms of manipulation are so well orchestrated that they appear to be natural. Schiller adds:

> When successfully employed, as they invariably are, the result is individual passivity, a state of inertia that precludes action. This, indeed, is the condition for which the media and the system-at-large energetically strive, because passivity assures the maintenance of the status quo. Passivity feeds upon itself, destroying the capacity for social action that might change the conditions that presently limit human fulfillment. (Schiller, 1973: 29)

Propaganda has a significant impact on the structuring of identities. As novelist Gore Vidal puts it: "Persuading the people to vote against their own best interests has been the awesome genius of the American political elite from the beginning" (quoted in Schiller, 1973: 2). Chomsky, commenting on the propaganda model states, "It is either valid or invalid. If invalid, it may be dismissed; if valid, it will be dismissed" (Chomsky, 1989: 11).

In the preface to *Necessary Illusions*, Chomsky describes the challenge that his work provides for critical thought:

> The issues that arise are rooted in the nature of Western industrial societies and have been debated since their origins. In capitalist democracies there is a certain tension with regard to the locus of power. In a democracy the people rule, in principle. But decision-making power over central areas of life resides in private hands, with large-scale effects throughout the social order. One way to resolve the tension would be to extend the democratic system to investment, the organization of work, and so on. That would constitute a major social revolution, which, in my view at least, would consummate the political revolutions of an earlier era and realize some of the libertarian principles on which they were partly based. Or the tension could be resolved, and sometimes is, by forcefully eliminating public interference with state and private power. In the advanced industrial societies the problem is typically approached by a variety of measures to deprive democratic political

structures of substantive content, while leaving them formally intact. A large part of this task is assumed by ideological institutions that channel thought and attitudes within acceptable bounds, deflecting any potential challenge to established privilege and authority before it can take form and gather strength. The enterprise has many facets and agents. I will be primarily concerned with one aspect: thought control, as conducted through the agency of the national media and related elements of the elite intellectual culture. (Chomsky, 1989: vii–viii)

To work critically, to act critically, to live critically within the communities of this society or any other compels us to continually search the limitations and containments of our own minds and experiences. In doing so, we must keep the relationship between theory and practice, as well as the relationship between injustice and disadvantage, constantly at the forefront of our description, analysis, and reconstruction of social reality.

bell hooks

bell hooks extends the work of both Freire and Chomsky. Her critical, inclusive feminism articulates the intersection of race, class, and gender, demanding a theoretical comprehension of our everyday, lived experience, a necessary step if we are to begin to live within a liberatory dynamic. While Chomsky speaks of thought control, hooks finds that "a culture of domination necessarily promotes addiction to lying and denial," which precludes the possibility of "a revolution of values":

That lying takes the presumably innocent form of many white people (and even some black folks) suggesting that racism does not exist anymore, and that conditions of social equality are solidly in place that would enable any black person who works hard to achieve economic self-sufficiency. Forget about the fact that capitalism requires the existence of a mass underclass of surplus labour.... individuals are not just presented untruths, but are told them in a manner that enables most effective communication. When this collective cultural consumption of and attachment to mis-information is coupled with the layers of lying individuals do in their personal lives, our capacity to face reality is severely diminished as is our will to intervene and change unjust circumstances. (hooks, 1994:29)

hooks (who, in the quote at the beginning of this chapter, said she came to theory because she "was hurting") warns: "Theory is not inherently healing, liberatory, or revolutionary. It fulfills this function only when we ask that it do so and direct our theorizing towards this end" (hooks, 1994: 61). Much of contemporary popular culture seems to attempt to placate or anaesthetize any critical or analytical response to the hurt of injustice. Ideology plays a fundamental part in this placation in what Freire calls the "culture of silence," Chomsky calls "thought control" or "manufacturing consent," and hooks calls "lying and denial."

hooks also demands that we rethink, or indeed reconfigure, our understanding of racism, by renaming this form of discrimination within society. She suggests that identifying this act in society as an expression of "White, Supremacist, Capitalist, Patriarchy" will provide a more realistic understanding. These words take us more effectively into the deep structural relationships that are at work within the discriminatory structures and interactions in society.

What this means is that we must attempt to combine our individual and collective understandings regarding the manipulation of our lives by ideological formations. We must recognize the need to maintain a continuing dialogue with others in an effort to perceive the systemic, structural aspects of society's creation of advantage for some and disadvantage for others.

The Masking of Social Reality

One of the reasons that the masking of social reality—and the subsequent deflection of critical attention away from transformative policy—is so effective is that the "ideology of individualism" has become so clearly embedded in our everyday reading and reckoning of social, political, and economic events. Joe Feagin summarizes the basic tenets of this ideology:

1. Each individual should work hard and strive to succeed in competition with others.
2. Those who work hard should be rewarded with success (seen as wealth, property, prestige, and power).
3. Because of widespread and equal opportunity, those who work hard will in fact be rewarded with success.
4. Economic failure is an individual's own fault and reveals lack of effort and other character defects. (quoted in Bolaria, 1995: 3)

To individualize experience, to create subjectivities that buy into such ideological views of social and economic distribution of reward and failure, is a method, as Dorothy Smith might say, for making sure that people do not know the social and economic determinants or influences in their everyday lives. The coup is, therefore, an experience for which the public is readied, primed, and lubricated—we open ourselves to our own exploitation. Readiness, in this sense, is in some ways logically parallel to what educational theorists describe as the "pre-alienation" of workers through the schooling experience, meaning that the citizen is readied ideologically to participate in his or her own mystification. (See Apple, 1982; Giroux, 1981; Willis, 1981.)

Although it may seem unusual to explore the concept of **conspiracy theory** within this context, it is crucial to comprehend its nature in addressing the impact of ideology upon our everyday life.

Conspiracy theory within both the academic community and the general public is often expressed in the same syntactical construction that people use when formulating racist comments: "I'm not racist, but..." becomes "I'm not suggesting a conspiracy theory or a conspiracy, but..." We find it interesting that in both cases these expressions are most often indicators that the opposite view is about to be forwarded. In conspiracy theory, the phrase is so well-used and so taken-for-granted that it needs some profound examination if we are not to be foolishly blind to its underlying frame or the process of its framing in our understanding:

Conspiracy theory: The theory that effects which fall to the benefit of some class (usually the ruling class) are produced by conspiracy of that class. Often attributed to Marxists, the conspiracy theory is in fact precisely what Marx's theory of history was designed to replace, by showing that the benefit of a ruling class will be secured, in the short term, independently of the intention to secure it, and despite any (benevolent) intention to relinquish it. (Scruton, 1982: 92)

There are two aspects to this definition that need attention. First, what is precisely meant by the term conspiracy? And, second, from the structuralist point of view, is there a structure (i.e., the means of production within a particular historical period) which produces or constructs advantage independent of the intentions of a particular group? In other words, does the structure itself transcend or override the advantage to persons or classes? It is interesting to note that, "to conspire" by definition literally means "to breathe together." There is a kind of political intimacy projected from this moment of definition that is not entirely without humour. But, as one further moves into the definition, conspiracy takes on a pejorative meaning:

to combine privily to do something criminal, illegal, or reprehensible (esp. to commit treason or murder, excite sedition, etc.) to plot .... to concur, to combine as by intention. (Oxford Universal Dictionary, 1933: 377)

We argue that one of the reasons that so many are so reticent to "stand with" or proffer a conspiracy theory perspective is that it makes contemporary systems of government, economic systems, technical systems, and most everything else appear "criminal, illegal, or reprehensible." To be that critical of the status quo does seem seditious. Not to be capable of seeing and responding to the "criminal, illegal, or reprehensible" because of its ideological clothing is, indeed, an example of the masking, numbing, and lobotomized politics that envelops much of our everyday reality. It is an expression of our narcosis. One of the reasons that difficulty arises in events that might be characterized by conspiracy theory is that the imputation of intent either to one group or to others in general is seen as projection; that is, connections or relations are speculated about rather than revealed through evidence. "To breathe together": do not such groups as doctors, teachers, and business people "breathe together" with intent to perform some action, such as healing, teaching, and selling? If we begin to ask such questions, which recognize the intent, we can also recognize the relational, coordinated, and linked frames within which these "conspiracies" arise in the semantic sense.

> So was the coup engineered by the BCNI [Business Council on National Issues] and its allies a conspiracy? For sociologist Patricia Marchak, a lot depends on how the term "conspiracy" is being used. If, by conspiracy, we mean a gathering of big business interests to more effectively influence, if not direct, government policy making, then the answer is "yes." But if conspiracy means a secret, clandestine operation plotted by big business to seize control of the reins of government in Ottawa, then the answer is "no." In general, the plans of the BCNI and its allies have been relatively transparent. (Clarke, 1997: 107)

So, is there a masking of social, political, and economic realities or is there a lack of critical access to the machinations of day-to-day policy construction by citizens within democracies? Our response is "yes" to both parts of this question. As we have just discussed, such maskings frequently take place within newspapers, television, and radio where public perceptions on social issues are systematically being shaped and reshaped to suit powerful interest groups in the society,. This structuring of information occurs within the agenda-setting mode of the media, whereby certain issues and events are rated for omission or inclusion for dissemination. When information about social, economic, and political issues do get filtered through, it is usually presented as unproblematic to the extent that individuals are unable to participate effectively in decisions that affect them.

We often see self-interest theory, **structural theory**, and conspiracy theory as counter-pointed bases for analysis. Indeed, the self-interest theory avoids an entire aspect of human activity—the historical record of humankind, of people who work together, pull together, "breathe together" to achieve common goals. In *The Radical Future of Liberal Feminism*, Zillah Eisenstein offers a counterpoint to the self-interest theory:

Today's feminists either do not discuss a **theory of individuality** or they unself-consciously adopt the competitive, atomistic ideology of liberal individualism. There is much confusion on this issue in the feminist theory we discuss here. Until a conscious differentiation is made between a *theory of individuality* that recognizes the importance of the individual within the social collectivity and the *ideology of individualism* that assumes a competitive view of the individual, there will not be a full accounting of what a feminist theory of liberation must look like in our Western society. (Eisenstein, 1981: 5)

This distinction is profound. It establishes and recognizes the power of both the individual and the social collectivity. Indeed, it allows us to move conceptually to new terrain regarding the tension between these two theories. Theory can generate possibilities and the renewal of a human being's critical aspects; ideologies diminish and mystify the complexities that all of us must face.

CHAPTER 5

The Representation and Reproduction of Race, Gender, and Class

> The essential history of the introduction of *class*, as a word which
> would supersede older names for social divisions, relates to the increas-
> ing consciousness that social position is made rather than merely
> inherited. All the older words, with their essential metaphors of stand-
> ing, stepping and arranging in rows, belong to a society in which posi-
> tion was determined by birth. Individual mobility could be seen as
> movement from one *estate, degree, order* or *rank* to another. What was
> changing consciousness was not only increased individual mobility,
> which could be largely contained within the older terms, but the new
> sense of a SOCIETY (q.v.) or a particular *social system* which actually
> created social divisions, including new kinds of division. (Williams,
> 1976: 52; emphasis in original)

"The modern idea of class," Jeremy Seabrook writes, "was born in Europe, became an obsession in Britain and was denied in the United States" (and, we might add, Canada). Today, he notes, the still-persistent "institutionalized social injustice ... is discussed in terms of 'inequality' rather than of opposing social classes" (Seabrook, 2002: 10-11).

In recent years, the concepts of gender and race have undergone simi-
lar shifts of meaning, moving away from biological determinism towards explanations based on social constructions. Within contemporary femi-
nism, for instance, the dominant conceptualization of women's social condition was, for some time, that all women were oppressed by men and that solidarity among women was a necessary precondition for overcoming

this oppression (for example, see Friedan, 1963; Millet, 1970). This approach asserted the "commonality, indeed of universality and primacy of female oppression" (King, 1997: 228–29). What it overlooked was not just the institutionalized nature of the oppression experienced by women—the structured inequalities—but also the diverse nature of the oppression—how, for instance, race, gender, class, and even religious oppression intersect. Arguing from the perspective of women of colour, Audre Lorde points out, "It is a particular academic arrogance to assume any discussion of feminist theory in this time and in this place without examining our differences, and without a significant input from poor women, black and Third World women, and lesbians" ((Lorde, 1983: 98); also see Gayle, 1992: 239). As for the question of class, Caroline Ramazanoglu concludes: "Social class creates both divisions between women in the course of our daily lives and also divisions between feminists in their interpretations of where women's political interests lie" (Ramazanoglu, 1989: 96).

"Race" has similarly become a contested concept. For many social theorists, enclosing the term within quotation marks is not enough; from their perspective, it needs to be removed from the discourse entirely. It has become recognized within the social sciences that the term has no scientific legitimacy; it is a social construction, an arbitrary term used to classify human beings, usually on the basis of skin colour. The danger in this, Victor Satzewich notes, is that if race is defined "as a label with no analytical utility, social scientists end up denying the reality of racism," which means "undermining the anti-racist struggle" (Satzewich, 1998: 30).

Here we use the term "race" while recognizing that, firstly, it is indeed a social construction that has in the past been presented, falsely, as having a scientific basis. We also recognize that the concept of race, although not always referring to physical characteristics (phenotype), is most often used as a distinction relating to people of colour or **visible minorities** and that the term "ethnicity" is now often used as a substitute for race.

Despite the shifts in meaning, a tendency remains in the discourse surrounding all of these concepts; the experiences of individuals within a given racial, gender, and class category are often still seen as being monolithic. Racial, gender, and class stereotypes permeate society and manifest themselves at all levels. Inside such a monolith, dominant voices control the discussions, and the less dominant voices are marginalized. The production and reproduction of race, gender, and class distinctions play a powerful role in people's everyday experiences.

Any consideration of the impact of the representation of race, gender, and class has to take into account the reality of the prevailing social hierarchy and how it is maintained through social institutions that serve to construct and reinforce our sense of identity, by way of both systematic and random or incidental representations.

The debates, and the actual events that are their fodder, can also involve the processes of racialization—actions, behaviours, or ideas that make race central in the construction of social relations. Racialization may not in itself be racist, yet it clearly situates the concept of race and ethnicity within a particular social domain or discourse. Sociologist Sherene H. Razack describes the process of racialization in the telling of Canadian history:

> Mythologies or national stories are about a nation's origins and history. They enable citizens to think of themselves as part of a community, defining who belongs and who does not belong to the nation. The story of the land as shared and as developed by enterprising settlers is manifestly a racial story. Through claims to reciprocity and equality, the story produces European settlers as the bearers of civilization, while simultaneously trapping Aboriginal people in the pre-modern, that is, before civilization has occurred. … If Aboriginal people are consigned forever to an earlier space and time, people of colour are scripted as late arrivals, coming to the shores of North America long after much of the development has occurred. (Razack, 2002: 2–3)

Thus, part of the problem revolves around the privileging of events, issues, and, indeed, "the constitution of spaces" (Razack, 2002: 1). In its early stages, second-wave feminist discourse, shaped by the structures of White male hegemony, was dominated by an articulate group of White middle-class women. This perspective developed the taken-for-granted notion that those women's experiences of gender oppression were somehow representative of the experiences of all women. Their analyses of women's social condition, for instance, took their own privileged experiences as the reference point for all women. As hooks points out:

> Privileged feminists have largely been unable to speak to, with, and for diverse groups of women because they either do not understand fully the inter-relatedness of sex, race and class oppression or refuse to take this inter-relatedness seriously. Feminist analyses of women's lot tend to focus exclusively on gender and do not provide a solid foundation on which to construct feminist theory. They reflect the dominant tendency in Western patriarchal minds to mystify women's reality by insisting that gender is the sole determinant of woman's fate. (hooks, 1984: 14)

Deborah King agrees that a problem arises when the focus is primarily on gender and adds:

> While contending that feminist consciousness and theory emerged from the personal, everyday reality of being female, the reality of millions of women was ignored. The phrase "the personal is the political" not only reflects a phenomenological approach to women's liberation—that is, of women defining and constructing their own reality—but also has come to describe the politics of imposing and privileging a few women's personal lives over all women's lives by assuming that these few could be prototypical. (King, 1997: 228–29)

The privileging of issues relating to White middle-class women is certainly not unique given the structure of society. Although they perceive of themselves as belonging to a subordinate group because of their sex, White women belong to society's dominant group as a result of their race and class, and they largely share the assumptions of this group. Their structural position, which is ideologically shaped, results in substantial social benefits.

Employment equity programs in Canada and the **affirmative action** programs in the United States have, for instance, delivered most of their benefits, limited as they may be, to White women. Considering the struggles leading up to the passing of the 1964 *Civil Rights Act* and the 1965 *Voting Rights Act* in the United States, Kathleen Cleaver found:

> Despite appropriating legal gains paid for in blood during the civil rights era, and benefiting in great numbers from legislation banning employment discrimination, white women, who represent the dominant force of American feminists, seem nearly inaudible in their opposition to racism. The perceptions that motivated the radical feminists, Third World feminists, and progressive women devoted to ending racial oppression have become peripheral among leading feminist authors. (Cleaver, 1997: 35)

The advantages gained by White women over the past 30 years have been obscured within a discourse that ignores historical socio-economic inequalities and, in its stead, revolves around the rhetoric of a society preoccupied with individual merit.

The phenomenon of reproduction (of consciousness, social norms, and values) within society comes into play, once again, through key social institutions. Among the major forces of socialization—the means by which individuals internalize various ideologies—are the education system and the mass media. The ideas disseminated by these institutions are reproduced and reinforced through informal everyday practices, and, because they are internalized, it is almost as if they aren't there at all. As Herbert Marcuse emphasizes, "This absorption of ideology into reality does not however, signify the 'end of ideology.' On the contrary, in a specific sense advanced industrial culture is more ideological than its predecessor, inasmuch as today the ideology is in the process of production itself" (Marcuse, 1964: 11, summarizing Theodor Adorno).

The Myth of Education as Social Equalizer

Education is usually considered to be the great equalizer, the institution that works to level out social inequalities within society. But the reality is that schools tend to reflect and reproduce the unequal social class system of the wider society (Bowles & Gintis, 1976). Educational opportunities are not the same for everyone; a person's social class can determine the quality of education received. Students with parents who earn high incomes tend to live in neighbourhoods with well-equipped public schools; they have access to expensive private schools; and the student-teacher ratio is more amenable to learning. There are exceptions, of course, where parents in lower-income areas make efforts to get their children into good public schools or make sacrifices to send their children to private schools. In some cases, smart children from ill-equipped schools sometimes beat the odds.

Schooling is, of course, a major beginning point for integration into the wider society and for forming understandings that later become taken for granted. For example, our conceptualizations of democracy, collective and individual rights, citizenship, and, indeed, the organization of authority and power in society are all introduced in schools, though these matters are seldom questioned or explored there on a deeper level. If education and schooling are to have democratic understandings of citizenship as a primal underpinning, children will need to experience democratic relationships with each other within public institutions. To take the economically advantaged out of an educational environment weakens the educational experience of all.

The other factor in the failure of schools to equalize is what has become known as the hidden or covert curriculum—the social relations of schooling. Students acquire certain skills in informal ways appropriate to the needs of capitalist society. Early on, they learn that the power relationships within schools are controlled more often by males than females; that children's power and authority to generate knowledge and participate in the construction of relationships are not only limited but are, for the most part, non-existent; and that, given the nature of capitalism, individualism and competitiveness are encouraged above other qualities. In general, many critics agree that too much competitiveness or too little of it can both be a problem and that moderation through co-operation is something to strive for and can be achieved through team sports, which represent a regular part of the school curriculum. It is within the hidden curriculum that racist, sexist, homophobic, and class-based stereotypes are often manifested and reinforced. Even unintentional messages delivered during interactions between teachers and students can establish an unequal power situation; un-monitored messages that pass among students in the playground can unsettle relationships.

Like the home environment, the school environment can have an impact on the objectives that students form in planning for their future place in society. Studies have shown the influence of social class on how little or how well informed students are about the preparation necessary for entering and being successful at university or other post-secondary endeavours. But race or ethnicity also plays a part, according to the 1992 Ontario Women's Directorate:

> Educational success is also correlated to race and to a lesser extent ethnicity. While a 1991 student survey undertaken by the Toronto Board of Education discovered that being foreign-born was no impediment to educational achievement, a high proportion of students at risk of leaving high school without a diploma came from Aboriginal (46 per cent), Black (36 per cent), Portuguese (33 per cent), and Hispanic (38 per cent) families. In comparison, being female is no longer an impediment to educational success, although males and females continue to follow different educational paths, which sustain gender segregation in the paid labour force. (Quoted in Naiman, 1997: 281)

In the legal profession women still tend to be concentrated in the area of family law, while in medicine they tend to move into family practice. In academia, fewer females than males are full professors or deans, and in business the situation is similar: fewer females than males are chief executive officers.

Today, with the cutbacks in education funding, major corporations are endeavouring to fill the gap by sponsoring educational projects and/or offering "free" computers and television sets to schools. At the same time, they see these schools as important advertising grounds for their products; hence, these free computers and televisions usually come with a price, that of the inclusion of advertising beneficial to the donor corporation. Advertising is also now creeping into the contents of textbooks: *The New York Times* (March 21, 1999) reported the case of a high-school mathematics textbook that used, unnecessarily, the names of commercial products in its examples. When confronted regarding their complicity in advertising to a captive audience, the authors responded with surprise that their efforts to introduce familiar cultural products into the learning environment could even be questioned.

Media Representations and Their Impact

As Joanne Naiman asserts, "While the family and the schools are certainly important agents of socialization, the mass media in the 20th century have come to be the most important means through which the dominant ideology is transmitted and maintained" (Naiman, 1997: 287). Given the enormous power of corporate media in disseminating information, information system managers are able to set the agenda in ranking issues as priorities for public consumption. In his research into information delivery, Chomsky identifies many crucial issues that disappear into what he calls the "black hole"—the dumping ground for the news or topics that media managers consider to be unfit for public consumption (Chomsky, 1999: 135).

Today, with the breaking down of national borders through international corporate takeovers, the penetration of advertising agencies into a country's marketing system, and mergers and trade organizations such as the WTO (**World Trade Organization**, previously known as GATT, the General Agreement on Tariffs and Trade) and treaties such as NAFTA (North American Free Trade Agreement), global élites are increasingly gaining even further control over important information. Indeed, domains of thought that were at one time communicated within family face-to-face interactions or within communities by people known to each other are now delegitimized or discounted. Everything from portrayals of **nationalism** to understandings of sexuality and/or sexual orientation to how to treat friends or others with respect are given legitimacy or shifted to new ground within TV advertising. Community or neighbourhood encounters centre on "meal-deal lunches," which are assumed to add value and legitimacy to, for instance, a father's time with his son after a Saturday morning soccer match. These TV messages serve a corporate agenda rather than represent an authentic family, community, or neighbourhood reality. **Transnational corporations** purvey monopolized and prepackaged forms of knowledge, and control over intellectual properties has become increasingly commodified (see Shiva, 1997, regarding the patenting and commodification of locally grown seeds by transnational corporations such as Monsanto and Cargill, thereby appropriating peasant knowledge and resources).

Canadian society has long been inundated with American information and entertainment: magazines and books, TV programs, movies, music, and sports. The easy access to cable distribution and Internet systems only increases the domination. Not surprisingly, American issues and the American political agenda often become a focus for the Canadian audience. In many instances, these issues—for example, the debates around the constitutional right of American citizens to bear arms—are not particularly pertinent to Canadians.

Consider the difference in the American and Canadian political systems as they relate to issues such as multiculturalism and employment equity. The United States has three recognized major cultural groups: Caucasian, African American, and Hispanic. The distinctiveness of these groups became most apparent during the protracted struggles of African Americans and the State culminating with the *Civil Rights Act* of 1964. Although Native Americans had and continue to have political differences with the State, they are marginalized to such an extent that they are usually not included in the prevailing political discourse.

In Canada, First Nations peoples are a recognized group that has moved to the front stage of Canadian public affairs. Although they have been discriminated against historically and have engaged more recently in a continuing struggle with the federal government, particularly over land claims, many Canadians have become somewhat aware of their issues and concerns. In Canada, other ethnic groups are organized around issues of language, racism, immigration, and credential transference. These groups are officially supported through the multicultural policy introduced by the federal government in 1971. The prime minister at the time, Pierre Elliott Trudeau, declared in the House of Commons that a multiculturalism policy would be based on four principles:

First, resources permitting, the government will seek to assist all Canadian cultural groups that have demonstrated a desire and effort to continue to develop a capacity to grow and contribute to Canada, and a clear need for assistance, the small and weak groups no less than the strong and highly organized.

Second, the government will assist members of all cultural groups to overcome cultural barriers to full participation in Canadian society.

Third, the government will promote creative encounters and interchange among all Canadian cultural groups in the interest of national unity.

Fourth, the government will continue to assist immigrants to acquire at least one of Canada's official languages in order to become full participants in Canadian society. (Quoted in Palmer, 1975: 136)

Notwithstanding these principles—which, when announced by the prime minister, drew a rare, unanimous, positive approval from the leaders of all the opposition parties—gender, race, and class inequalities have persisted in Canada through the three decades since the policy was introduced. In practice, the policy's principles have been translated into the promotion of diverse cultural activities rather than into addressing more urgent socio-political issues (see Bannerji, 1991, 1995; Brand, 1993). Visible minorities, for example, have continued to be concentrated in low-paying, menial, dead-end jobs. As Michael Buraway notes, "Any work context involves an economic dimension (production of things), a political dimension (production of social relations), and an ideological dimension (production of an experience of those relations)" (Buraway, 1985: 39). Making those relationships clear calls for a critical, public examination.

The principle that the government would continue to assist non-English/non-French-speaking immigrants to acquire at least one of Canada's official languages as an aid to full participation in society, though well-intentioned, is fraught with problems. The government has supported second-language programs, but employers are still reluctant to hire their graduates, who find it difficult to integrate into the workforce. Quebec avoided this problem for many years, since early immigrants who settled there tended to come from the French-speaking areas of Europe and integrated fairly well into Quebec society. Today, most French-speaking immigrants come from French-speaking areas of Africa and the Caribbean, and the problem now centres on racial integration. In some ways this shift in immigration mirrors tendencies elsewhere in Canada.

A 1998 report on immigration added to the problems. It included a wide range of recommendations that could have a severe impact on the principles of multiculturalism. One proposed that new immigrants should come to Canada already equipped with one of the two official languages, and, that if they are not so equipped, the onus should fall on them to acquire it—a huge stumbling block given that most new immigrants to Canada now come from Asia and Latin America and are usually not fluent in either of the official languages. After being criticized over the years on issues of immigration and immigrant adjustment programs, the Canadian federal government intervened by establishing employment equity policies in government institutions. These advocate the hiring of qualified White women, First Nations people, people with disabilities, and visible minorities. As Brym notes, these "policies and programs seek to dismantle barriers and alter workplace cultures in order to create opportunities for and to further the advancement of historically disadvantaged groups" (Brym, 2001: 206). However, the policies do not extend to the private sector, except on a voluntary basis, which limits the possibilities for expansion of the goals.

As limited as they are, the employment equity programs have come under constant attack. A First Nations writer, Patricia A. Monture, counters what she sees as a basic misunderstanding of discrimination: "Critics of affirmative action describe these programs as reverse discrimination. I do not believe in such a phenomenon because to discriminate we must first wield power. Logically, those without power cannot meaningfully discriminate" (Monture, 1993: 335).

Media and the Depoliticization of Social Issues

The progress experienced by White women and minorities in the wider society, despite limitations, has not been completely reflected in popular media images. Rather, a media system whose primary agenda is making profits through advertisements rather than exposing racial and gender inequalities has compounded the problems. The labour force represented in TV ads and situation comedies, for example, has consistently shown little relationship to what studies show are the real-life employment patterns of women and other minorities. In advertisements, despite decades of feminism, women continue to be objectified, used mainly to sell products, rather than being portrayed as complicated, complete human beings. Advertisers have managed to distort the messages of the second-wave women's movement to their own advantage—adopting slogans for cigarette ads such as "You've come a long way baby"; for hosiery, "The revolutionary pantyhose"; or, for gasoline advertisements, superimposing the heads of revolutionaries such as Angela Davis on other people's bodies (see the films "Killing Us Softly 3" [Kilbourne, 2000] and "Ways of Seeing" [Berger, 1974]).

Male and female racial minorities tend to be clustered together as a homogeneous group and presented as Other, making it even more difficult to articulate a distinction between gender and racial oppression. News reports, movies, advertisements, cartoons, TV sitcoms, and fiction perpetuate certain images: in the realm of politics minorities are, for the most part, either exoticized or demonized, or both at the same time; they are consistently portrayed as being powerless and, therefore, as of little political concern (see O'Neale, 1986; hooks, 1992; Hoberman, 1997). Their life experiences tend to be presented as social pathology, far removed from actual social and economic contexts.

Further perpetuating the idea of the Other as powerless is the tendency of broadcasters or journalists to call on racial minorities only when the issues being examined are race-related. In this way, the industry assumes a certain level of ignorance on the part of minorities of issues not based solely on questions of race, as if minorities are somehow unable to grasp the essence of environmental issues, or structural adjustment programs, or constitutional questions, or other such matters. Racial minorities, thus, become ghettoized in the media world, and issues become racialized in the wider world. Homi Bhabha emphasizes this notion. The media, he says, call "on people of colour to represent divergent political positions on various issues so long as their diversity is contained by a kind of ideological and political matrix that always makes them into little nations. They have to be subnations. They have to see their context as subnational" (Bhabha, 1999: 26).

As mentioned earlier, in his book *Covering Islam*, Edward Said points out that the representation of the Muslim world in the West has been based on misinformation rather than information. Again, the events of September 11, 2001, have demanded that the West begin to understand the multiplicity of Islamic traditions and societies. Islam, like any other religious ideology, manifests itself in different forms, depending on the particular societal histories of different populations, yet representations of it continue to reflect a monolithic approach. Similar misrepresentations also occur in terms of how we understand women in the Third World.

According to Ghanaian writer Ama Ata Aidoo, images of the passive, victimized African woman are often created out of good intentions, such as the Bob Geldof Band Aid concert, organized to raise money for the victims of the famine in Ethiopia. She draws attention to the standard image, which portrays the African woman as having too many children for whom she cannot adequately care. The woman and her children are hungry. Aidoo points out that it has become a cliché of Western journalism that the African woman is old beyond her years, half-naked, with a permanent begging bowl in her hand, while flies buzz around the faces of her children (Aidoo, 1992: 1–7; see also Gayle, 1998:45).

Such representations persist because they have proven to be powerful marketing tools for major advertising campaigns. In the film *Developing Images* (International Broadcasting Trust, 1988), an administrator from the Save the Children Fund argues that her organization deliberately presents people who seem to be in need, because if North Americans see healthy-looking people on the screen or on the pages of magazines, they might not be inclined to make donations. As a rule the media presentation of what is modern, institutionalized poverty, calling for private donations of assistance for people who have been historically colonized into institutionalized poverty, carries no recognition of the historical roots of the problems. As William K. Carroll suggests, "Should we not be asking why it is that problems of endemic poverty get addressed through private fund-raising, 'outside' the circuitry of capital but within the televisual circuits of mass media?" (Carroll, 2001). Such media images have an enduring effect, and, unfortunately, most North American consumers of those images have been left to make sense of the world through them.

"The Other": Intersections and Transformations

hooks, considering the context of the ideology of domination, argues, "As subjects people have the right to define their own reality, establish their own identities, name their history. As objects, one's reality is defined by others, one's identity created by others, one's history named only in ways that define one's relationship to those who are subjects" (hooks, 1988: 42–43). So long as the prevailing construction of domination and subordination persists in North America, those perceived as subordinate will remain objects, and, as objects, they will continue to be manipulated by the dominant society. For example, Lorde explained that, when women of colour were included on women's conference panels in the early 1980s, they were usually called at the last minute; when confronted about this problem, organizers would say, as an excuse, that they didn't know whom to call. Lorde also cited the editorial practice of journals that described their publications as special issues when they dealt with the art or writing of women of colour (Lorde, 1983: 100). In other words, issues pertaining to women of colour were merely added on rather than made central to various projects. Much the same situation applied in women's studies programs; in many instances, the works of women of colour were usually not even on reading lists, much less on lists of required texts. Lorde calls this a form of subtle racism. Himani Bannerji uses her own, more recent, experience to detail the same divide:

> In curriculum meetings, in designing courses white men and women automatically spoke about "theory" and Marxism and feminism as their preserve. I was allowed to speak to an "issue," racism not being seen as a fundamental form of social organization of what is called "Canada" and thus not an entry point into social analysis. To this day I get invited to lecture on this "issue" of racism once or twice in courses

on feminist or social theory. Not even feminist theorists of the left seem to know how to build in this "issue" as an integral aspect of their theoretical/analytical enterprise. (Bannerji, 1995: 110)

In high schools too, the same problem appears. Advocates for the addition of women's studies programs to the curriculum apparently do not envision an inclusive approach. The agenda is to get women's studies into the schools; after this goal is accomplished, the marginalized groups representing those categorized as "Others" will be added. Ironically, White feminists have levelled attacks at White male dominance in their arguments regarding the exclusion of White women from positions in major institutions. According to Angela Davis (1989), the structure of domination/subordination within the feminist movement is so entrenched that dominant feminists do not even recognize the power relationships involved when they invite women of colour to participate in events that result from activities that should have been collaborative in the first place. Feminists from the dominant class usually set the politico-feminist agenda; there is no toleration for deviation at either the conceptual level or the level of people's experiences.

For many of us, the goal of feminist, anti-racist, and anti-classist struggles is social transformation and social justice for all women. This calls for a better understanding of the diversity of women's concerns and experiences, which can only be achieved by listening to the voices of those who have been excluded, combined with a serious commitment to their full participation in the project. In the words of Hill Collins:

As the "Others" of society who can never really belong, strangers threaten the moral and social order. But they are simultaneously essential for its survival because those individuals who stand at the margins of society clarify its boundaries. African American women, by not belonging, emphasize the significance of belonging. (Hill Collins, 1990: 68)

Feminist analysis, therefore, must give centrality to issues of class and race. We must strive to develop what Dorothy Smith calls a **feminist**

epistemology: a method of thinking about women that starts from their actual lived experiences, a method that encompasses the variations in their experiences. In Afghanistan, after the defeat of the Taliban, Afghani women have asserted their power to shape the shifts and changes necessary to deal with the structures of their own lives. They have specifically demanded that Western women respect this right. As General Suhalia Siddiq stated, "The first priority should be given to education, primary school facilities, the economy and reconstruction of the country but the West concentrates on the burqa and whether the policies of the Taliban are better or worse than other regimes" (quoted in Farrell, 2001).

A new understanding will begin with the abandonment of assumptions and stereotypes and the demystification of ideological constructs through which "universal woman" is equated with "White women." This challenge, if taken up, could provide a model for the analyses of class and racial inequalities in society in general, an analysis that recognizes the intersection of race, gender, and class in the structuring of identity.

CHAPTER 6

Ideology and the Privatization of Public Policy

> You have a 1997 car. You want a 1997 road. And to do that, by economics of scale you need a larger community to pay. (Fyfe, 1998: D1)

> The ideology of the public/private dichotomy allows government to clean its hands of any *responsibility* for the state of the "private" world and *depoliticizes* the disadvantages which inevitably spill over the alleged divide by affecting the position of the "privately" disadvantaged in the "public" world. (Lacey, 1993: 97; emphasis in original)

The public/private configuration has been with us for centuries, in various guises, and remains with us now as a means of separating the concerns of everyday life from the supposedly larger concerns of governance and corporate affairs. The dichotomy, as ideology and reality, is everywhere, and it is everywhere full of contradictions. Family homes are the most obvious example of the private domain; the workplace is in the public domain. But as a public domain the factory, for instance, has always been seen as male, even when women entered into it as the economy demanded. The private domain, the home, was women's place, the domestic sphere. In addition to the factory and workshop, men also had the public worlds of business and political affairs to call their own.

The private spaces have not always been safe havens, especially for women and children; public spaces, too, have been less than welcoming to workers (i.e., injuries on the job, environmental hazards, and the lowest possible wages whenever possible) and to minority groups (the examples are numerous, but see, especially, James in Satzewich, 1998, on police in Toronto). Significantly, people often find it necessary to escape the private spaces in which they live, and many frequently hang out on street corners or in public parks. As Sherene Razack explains:

> For the tenant, the housing project may be experienced as racialized space in which communities of colour both experience their marginal condition and resist it. Perhaps people gather on street corners to socialize, defying the containment offered by the buildings and imagining them instead as symbols of community. (Razack, 2002: 9)

Other contradictions abound. The private sector is often referred to as the engine of the economy; the public sector is often considered to be wasteful and inefficient. But the private sector has not been able to deliver the goods to all citizens with anything close to equitable results; the public sector has been called on to fill the gaps, to provide the safety net. Pierre Elliott Trudeau, as Minister of Justice in 1968, declared "there's no place for the state in the bedrooms of the nation" (Woodcock, 1988: 381). But the state, since then, has moved both to regulate and to protect citizens within these sites.

Thus, the private/public dichotomy in itself has been yet another contested ideology, beset with conceptual and experiential intricacies. "Feminist analyses of this traditional public/private dichotomy have revealed it to be a contrived division, perpetuated to maintain patriarchal power.... Women of the working class, unmarried women, women who are single mothers, and lesbian mothers in co-parenting relationships have often had neither the means nor the desire to live as the dichotomy would dictate," argue the editors of *Changing Patterns: Women in Canada* (Burt, Code, & Dorney 1993: 10). Sociologist Mercedes Steedman points out: "Historians argue that the idea of men belonging to the public sphere and of women belonging to the private sphere originated in Enlightenment thought and in the middle-class male dominance of civil institutions of eighteenth-century society" (Steedman, 1997: 3). But even when women moved into work outside the home and achieved political gains such as the right to vote, their struggles against oppressions and inequalities were by no means over.

Personal, private, and individual space has, then, long been differentiated from common, collective, public domains. To experience public space involves an understanding that a particular space is not owned or sequestered, that it has common access, that it is supposedly unrestricted space—though perhaps it is not so much unrestricted as differently restricted or controlled by different rules or norms. The experience of what is considered private and what is considered public changes over time, too. For example, within the public/private division of space, people's experience and conceptualization of sexuality became more private as the domestic space of the home became more isolated. Yet at the same time, sexuality has now become increasingly public in the numerous ways in which it is expressed. The two domains and the subsequent organization of our life spaces have a kind of opposing power (see Foucault, 1978). Not only do our life spaces shift as social and cultural understandings of public/private space change, but how we think about these experiences and our perceptions of them also changes.

It is interesting to think about how children come to understand what is public and what is private in our communities. Indeed, the early conceptualizations formed about this divide are often never again questioned: they simply become part of the child's frame of reference, the child's ideological understanding of how space is distributed within communities. Questions arise, such as whose responsibility is it to clean up a particular space, who has the authority to be here or go there, and why can't I go there? These questions lead us into an investigation of the ideological underpinnings of this often taken-for-granted divide.

The ideological expressions, representations, and systems of belief are by definition not isolated, personal, or subjective in nature. Rather, ideologies occupy a public, though internalized, space that, without critical reflection on the part of individuals, or without the disclosure of public debate or public discourse, remains subject to the hidden forces of the public/private dichotomy. The questions around the role of ideology and the privatization of public policy lead us from the microlevel of everyday, community-based experience to the macrolevel contexts of the nation-state and global society.

The Public/Private Divide

Given the distinction, in economics and political affairs, of the public sector and the private sector, we might recall C. Wright Mills's perspective on the personal troubles of milieu and the public issues of social structure (Mills, 1959: 8; see Chapter 1, this volume). Mills's work relates to the concepts of public domain/private domain—a terrain that has a certain continuum.

FIGURE 6.1: Public Domain/Personal Domain

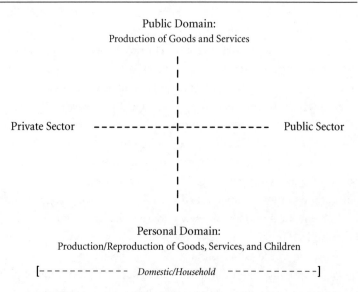

Over time this continuum becomes subject to historical shifts that alter the matrix.

Below the arrow added to the figure shows the trajectory of education and schooling both as it has moved over the past 150 years from the private home to the community's public domain and as it has been pushed more recently in the direction of the corporatized private sector. As Tony Clarke points out, both public and post-secondary schools have "become prime targets for corporate takeover":

FIGURE 6.2: The Public Domain/Personal Domain Continuum

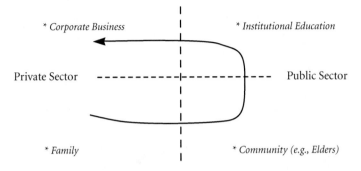

Public Domain:
Production of Goods and Services

Corporate Business   *Institutional Education*

Private Sector   Public Sector

Family   *Community (e.g., Elders)*

Personal Domain:
Production/Reproduction of Goods, Services, and Children

[- - - - - - - - - - - - *Domestic/Household* - - - - - - - - - - - -]

All over the country, deficit-driven provincial governments have been slashing education budgets, contracting out educational services, and exploring ways of privatizing pieces of the public education system. Cash-starved schools are increasingly turning to corporations to supply them with the technology, curriculum and food services they can no longer afford to buy. Coca Cola, McDonald's, Pepsi-Cola, Burger King, IBM, General Electric, Bell Canada and AT&T are a few of the brand name corporations which are more than ready to provide these services in exchange for the right to advertise their products in a captive youth market. (Clarke, 1997: 131)

More generally, we could also position various other institutions within society on the matrix. For example, on the horizontal axis, IBM or Nike are examples of private-sector, public-domain corporations just as a local, family-run restaurant is situated as a small business in the private sector. In Canada, Petro-Canada, Air Canada, and many other corporations, which used to belong to the public sector, have now been privatized. The vertical axis shows the difference between the private domain of one's own bedroom and the public domain of the local park. Using this grid, we can relate to our own experiences within these sites as we think through the public/private divide. Where and at what moments, for instance, do we act as a family member, or as a citizen, and where and at what moments do we act as a student, a worker (part or full time), or business person?

Ironically, after 20 years of neo-liberalism on the political landscape, with its highly charged demand to fight big government and thus avoid large deficits that, in the corporate mind, translate into heavy taxation on profits, the presence of government has never been so imposing—at least for the ordinary person. The imposition has arisen from a series of contradictions and twists—privatization and deregulation of state services and institutions, globalization of economic and social life, and the corporatization of all aspects of everyday existence. Rather than less government, we seem to have more—despite the ideologically implemented decreases in regulation and less government intervention in the market. The irony of the situation deepens given the well-documented corporate dependency on government. According to Gary Teeple: "Despite the popular assumption that business could manage well without government and would do better with less government, the corporate sector is hardly about to abandon these vital roles of the state, which support capital." Teeple elaborates on what has really happened:

> The attack on "big government" has essentially been an attack against any state intervention aimed at ameliorating the conditions of the working class or against a growing **politicization** of the distribution of the social product. "Big government" as an epithet is aimed at the welfare state but not at state support of corporations. Ignored in this aspersion are the gifts, grants and favours that have been extended to the business sector in the form of tax expenditures, inflated contracts, control of labour unions, legislative suppression of wages, socialization of production costs, social control, and creation of infrastructure. (Teeple, 2000: 47)

We have also experienced a fundamental shift in how we think about, and what we think of, these two central domains—the private and the public. Historically, the family was perceived as being in the private domain.

But the family home was also, always, a workplace, both for women who did domestic (and other) work and for men who were, for example, craft-workers or agriculturalists. Eventually, the domain of the family became most often the site of production, reproduction, and consumption, and the public domain was the site of work, business, and political life. The dichotomy tended, as we have seen, to be a gendered arrangement. But, as Susan B. Boyd notes, we need to take care not to "portray the public/private divide as a natural or determinate division. Whereas white women might complain about a historical lack of legal protection in the private sphere of family, Black women or Aboriginal women might protest that, in their families, state intervention has been all too prevalent" (Boyd, 1997: 13).

Again, the contradictions emerge and emphasize the distinctions: women might want both more state protection within the home—against marital assault, for instance—and less state intervention into their lives—for example, when it comes to their right to keep their children. Roberta Hamilton states:

> This gender polarity goes far beyond individual expressions of **masculinity** and femininity because it pervades the structuring of both private and public worlds and their separation from each other. The public world is supposed to be governed by notions of **instrumental rationality**—that is, the emphasis is on the most technically efficient means of reaching goals. Whether in the realm of bureaucracy, public policy, or multinational corporations, the preoccupation with this narrow form of rationality marks the public world as a stereotypical expression of "masculinity." All emotion, love, intimacy, caring, and nurturing are relegated to the private world of family and friendship, where they are marked as the special domain of women. (Hamilton, 1996: 190)

The designation of what is public versus what is private varies within society. In some instances, that which is public is regulated by the state; the historical movement of children's education from home to institutionalized schooling means that children and children's experience have become a public good. In others, the public space is regulated by or delegated to the employer. In some cases, it is set by stereotypes of colour or other ethnically based characteristics. Stereotyping and racist attitudes and acts are by definition public acts. To be of African descent is to be so publicly. A person's inner (subjective) experiences as well as external (objective) understandings and the conditions of the public/private divide are influenced by the ideological dimensions of everyday life.

The Boundaries of Everyday Life

The intimate domains of our own everyday lives at the microlevel contain a number of typical elements of daily life that in theory are subject to, or at least touched by, public or private relations. These elements are based both on historical circumstances and the contingencies of gender, race, and class.

FIGURE 6.3: The Elements of Daily Life

PUBLIC – PRIVATE

Children
Partners
Housework
Work
Food
Health
Sex
Sites of consumption/consumerism
Sport
Law
Knowledge
Library
Arts
Transportation
Entertainment
Information
Sound/noise
Property
Environment
Commons
Family
Religion
State
Schools
Prisons
Waste/Litter

Each of us has examples of experiences and/or activities that we can place on the graphic presentation of the horizontal and vertical axis. Which of these experiences do we have at home, and which outside the home? Which elements are publicly funded and/or provided, and which are privately funded and/or provided? What are the pros and cons of each of these means of provision? The possibilities are infinite, yet the shifts from public to private, or vice versa, appear to be continuous. For example, when did certain methods of transportation become public, and what conditions have determined levels of public transportation? Have sex and the sale of sex taken on new or different public meanings and expression? What do we consume publicly today that we historically consumed, and produced, at home? If we are living in the information age, where is knowledge or information located, and who has control over it? Are knowledge and information now consumable commodities? Clearly, these last three questions have been answered: those who have begun to work through the ideological clutter since 1991 now refer to the Gulf War as the War Against Iraq and document how information and news were filtered through American government channels before appearing in the Western media in order to present the government's view of events. Is the same thing happening again, as American government rhetoric adds momentum to a new war against Iraq and Saddam Hussein?

Here is another example: in contemporary business life, within the ultracompetitive arena of computer sales, has information or knowledge become a commodity? Say a person visits a computer store to gather necessary information and knowledge regarding specific needs, wants, and desires for a product from "live" salespeople as well as "live" hardware or software. This customer goes home, having garnered this knowledge, and uses it to order a new computer at a reduced price off the Internet. What is the power in terms of profitability of this new knowledge? Does this practice activate a new ethic regarding consumption?

One could illustrate this "use value" of information and knowledge within communities with the example of local baseball coaching knowledge or sport in general. The commodification of young athletes, as they and their parents reach for major league contracts, also means that knowledge related to sports player development becomes commodified within local communities. Huge sums of money are expended in order to get youngsters into élite programs or élite coaching, supposedly with a contract signing-bonus as the goal.

From the Public to the Private Economy

What role does ideology now play in the manufacture, commodification, control, distribution, and internalization of knowledge and information within various public or private social contexts? In addition, how does the public/private mix work itself out in the economic contexts of our everyday lives?

In her "three-layer cake (with icing)," Hazel Henderson (1995) provides a graphic representation of the dynamic of the public and private economies in an industrial society. Perhaps the most telling aspect of her model is the notion of dependence or reliance: the ingredients in each layer of the cake ultimately rely on (or are accountable/responsible to) the layer below. For instance, work traditionally undertaken by women—"sweat-equity"—is, to use Sylvia Hale's (1990) phrase, "sub-contracted work for the corporate sector." The ideological representations necessary to distort this sense of order—to develop the argument, for instance, that the "private sector is the engine of the economy"—lack credibility when natural resources, for instance, take a valid or valued position in a holistic formation. The dominant worldview suggests that we are dependent upon nature rather than being an integral part of it, or responsible to it.

Unfortunately, although the model implies a gender "ingredient," it falls short of including class and race in the mix. Henderson's cake explicates and locates much of our daily life experience within certain boundaries. We need also to consider how these boundaries are created and, in the light of her model, determine where or how the stream of advantage flows.

Significantly too (particularly in view of our understanding of socialization theory), the presentation of that which is public and that which is private is never directly or adequately addressed within our educational institutions. What should rightfully be held in common, and what should be left to the people who live within a community or

FIGURE 6.4: Total Productive System of an Industrial Society

(Three-Layer Cake with Icing)

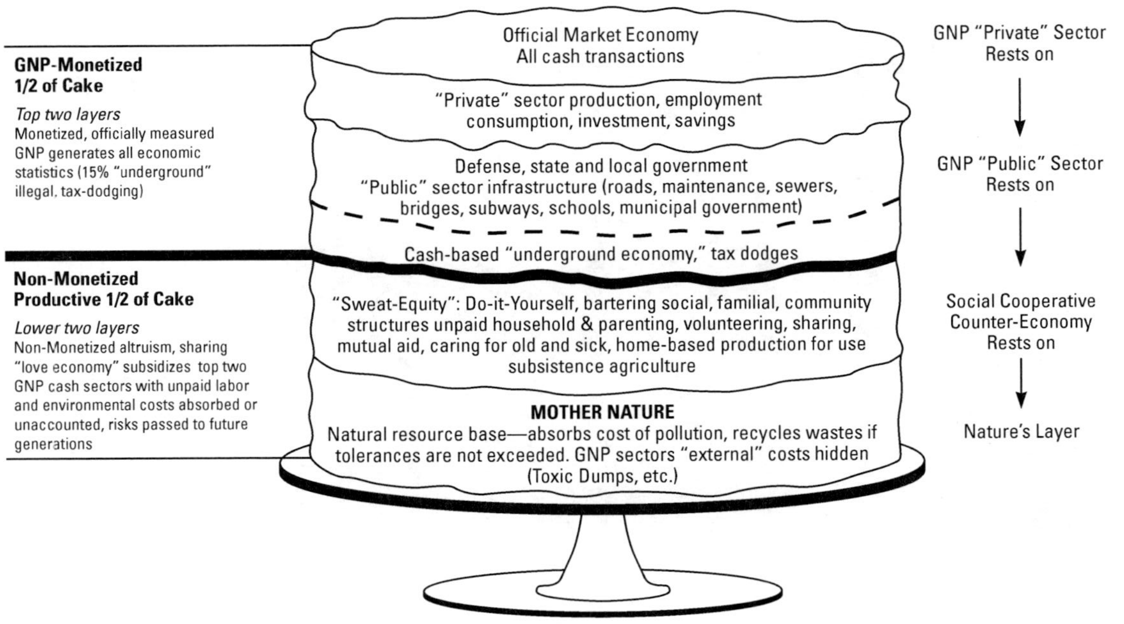

GNP "Private" Sector Rests on →

GNP "Public" Sector Rests on →

Social Cooperative Counter-Economy Rests on →

Nature's Layer →

Official Market Economy
All cash transactions

"Private" sector production, employment consumption, investment, savings

Defense, state and local government
"Public" sector infrastructure (roads, maintenance, sewers, bridges, subways, schools, municipal government)

Cash-based "underground economy," tax dodges

"Sweat-Equity": Do-it-Yourself, bartering social, familial, community structures unpaid household & parenting, volunteering, sharing, mutual aid, caring for old and sick, home-based production for use subsistence agriculture

MOTHER NATURE
Natural resource base—absorbs cost of pollution, recycles wastes if tolerances are not exceeded. GNP sectors "external" costs hidden (Toxic Dumps, etc.)

GNP-Monetized 1/2 of Cake

Top two layers
Monetized, officially measured GNP generates all economic statistics (15% "underground" illegal. tax-dodging)

Non-Monetized Productive 1/2 of Cake

Lower two layers
Non-Monetized altruism, sharing "love economy" subsidizes top two GNP cash sectors with unpaid labor and environmental costs absorbed or unaccounted, risks passed to future generations

family to decide? It is possible to build an entire school curriculum around the issue of the public/private dichotomy.

Globalization: Corporatization, Privatization, and Deregulation

Lorne Tepperman and Jenny Blain provide a concise basic understanding of a term that has become part of our everyday language: "Globalization is the increasing interdependence among the economies and societies of the world." They suggest, "The global economy is a form of world social organization with six defining features" (Tepperman & Blain, 1999: 188–89):

1. Global economic interdependence—that is, a single world market—means trade in goods and services with prices set simultaneously in hundreds of countries.
2. Scientific and technological innovation is a driving force in the economy.
3. Key actors in the global economy are "constructed" or corporate entities (such as GM, IBM, Toyota, Exxon).
4. Cultures and politics are polycentric, that is, located in and influenced by activities in many nations.
5. An evolving "world culture" homogenizes human aspirations, narrowing the variety of desires and lifestyles.
6. Globalization forces nation-states to adapt; that is, nation-states have less influence over local cultures and economies and less control over their own peoples.

The very term globalization is an interesting example of how a complex set of social, economic, and political forces can become quickly depoliticized. Once the word becomes part of our everyday speech, as it has over the last decade or so, its embedded ideological meaning fades away. The distant and abstract nature of globalization processes makes it difficult for people to see the relationship of the phenomena to their everyday lives. People respond in a different way to new forms of consumer choice, the corporatization (and loss) of jobs, and the cultural signs and representations (and institutions) in their communities. The expansion and contraction of diversity happens simultaneously, and the potential death of the nation-state comes closer. But this globalization is not all that new. Almost three decades ago, Richard Barnett and Ronald Müller wrote about the power of global corporations:

> In the process of developing a new world, the managers of firms like GM, IBM, Pepsico, GE, Pfizer, Shell, Volkswagen, Exxon, and a few hundred others are making daily business decisions which have more impact than those of most sovereign governments on where people live; what work, if any, they will do; what they will eat, drink and wear; what sorts of knowledge schools and universities will encourage; and what kind of society their children will inherit. (Barnett & Müller, 1974: 81–82)

Indeed, over the past 20 years the corporatization, privatization, and deregulation of many elements of our daily collective and individual lives have been extensive. For example, the corporatization of medical care, the privatization of educational institutions, and the deregulation of transportation systems have all altered the spaces in which we place ourselves and live out our experiences. As Warren Magnusson puts it:

> Much of what people have in mind when they talk about "globalization" is the intensification of market pressures, pressures that force open protected local markets and at the same time require people to sell what was not previously marketed. All activities—including artistic creation, scholarly research, charitable service, and public deliberation—are now considered to be marketable commodities, which ought to be supplied in the forms and quantities demanded by willing buyers. There are fewer and fewer places to escape from the dictates of the market, unless one has already been a success on the market, or can claim inherited wealth. To merit a decent life, one must have worth on the market, and to have worth on the market one must become what the market demands. (Magnusson, 1997: 107)

Some critics say that these processes are the result of neo-liberalism; others maintain that they are the result of economic or technological forces outside of the political landscape—that they are, as we so often hear, "inevitable." Some people say we have to accommodate ourselves to these conditions. Others say we have to resist them. Clearly, ideology plays a role in the acceptance of, or resistance to, these phenomena. For example, Clarke points out, the incursion of the private corporate sector into the public school system has ideological as well as practical implications:

> As education activist Jim Turk explains, corporations moving into the education field these days have three strategic objectives in mind. The first is to capture the youth market and a new generation of consumers. The second is to make the delivery of education more dependent on their corporate funds and products. The third is eventually to change the curriculum and the content of education programming in the schools. Says Turk: "The third objective is part of the corporate strategy of creating a more docile and subservient work force." (Clarke 1997: 131)

Central to this phenomenon in Canada has been the setting of the public agenda by the private corporate sector, in particular by think-tanks like the right-wing Fraser Institute or the powerful organization known as the Business Council on National Issues (BCNI), a lobby group composed of the chief executive officers of the leading corporations in the country. The BCNI has had a huge impact upon major issues such as the public debate regarding the Free Trade Agreement (FTA) and North American Free Trade Agreement (NAFTA). For Murray Dobbin, the BCNI's main objective since its establishment in the 1970s has been the transformation of public policy—so much so that through its task forces it has become "a virtual shadow cabinet":

> The task forces were established and dissolved according to the political priorities of the day. Among the task forces were those addressing national finance (that is, taxation), international economy and trade, social policy and regional development, labour relations and manpower, government organization and regulation, foreign policy

and defence, competition policy, education, and corporate governance.
(Dobbin, 1998: 167)

Alongside the corporatization and privatization of economic life is a two-pronged initiative, which is at least 20 years old now—the deregulation and downsizing of the nation-state (in effect the dismantling of the nation-state) and the dismantling of the welfare state. The privatization of what in the past were public domains—transportation systems, for example—and the commodification of certain social and public interests—such as the arts—added to the corporatization not just of the domains of production but also, now, of the domains of reproduction leads to a fundamental question: "What will a system of reproduction based primarily on the principles of the market mean for the future?" (Teeple, 2000: 4–5).

The State, Civil Society, and the Reproduction of the Modern Citizen

Since the beginning of the modern nation-state, perhaps one of the most enduring questions has been who is going to fund or provide for the production and reproduction of the citizen/worker. Marx, in the first volume of *Capital*, states: "If the owner of labour-power works today, tomorrow he must again be able to repeat the same process in the same conditions as regards health and strength. His means of subsistence must therefore be sufficient to maintain him in his normal state as a labouring individual" (Marx, 1967: 171).

Is the education, health, and social development of the individual the responsibility of the public, in this case the state, or is it the responsibility of the private resources available to the individual? Over the years the debate on this issue has meandered from one side of the political spectrum to the other, with tangled results. For example, if we have a state-funded health system, do we have a public responsibility to wear safety glasses when cutting concrete? When we take the liberty of skiing out of bounds in some remote mountain range, should we have to pay our own search and rescue or retrieval bills? If the corporate sector wants educated, literate workers, should that same sector be the source of educational funding for those potential workers? According to Marx, at least the wages (subsistence) need to be enough to "maintain and renew" the worker, to use Peter Li's (1996) phrasing.

Li's discussion of the "overhead cost of labour" in his book *The Making of Post-War Canada* demands that we reckon with the question of "who pays?" The worker arrives at the job as an already "produced commodity":

> But unlike the pre-capitalist economy in which the cost of labour renewal was met by pooling the labour of family members, the family in the capitalist market meets this cost by pooling the wages that family members bring home, and by relying on the unpaid domestic labour mainly performed by women. (Li, 1996: 31)

The resources for the "maintenance" (on a daily basis) and "renewal" (on a generational basis) (Li, 1996: 31) are indeed mixed within contemporary society. In Canada, education and health care are, to certain levels, state-provided and state-funded. But still, workers and their families bear much of the overhead cost of labour. The "fiscal crisis of the state" (Li, 1996: 91) and the "decline of the welfare state" (see Teeple, 2000) become ideologically entangled, and the act of disentangling becomes more and more difficult.

As Li notes, "Capital profits from the welfare state" and "the cost of financing the welfare state is socialized." Then, too, "The social surplus created in the capitalist economy is privatized" (Li, 1996: 91). In this supposed public/private divide, the citizenry bears the costs, while the private sector enjoys the rewards. However, within the past 20 to 30 years, the decline of the welfare state has precipitated a monumental off-loading of responsibility, most commonly onto the shoulders of women within the domestic domain. With an increasingly ageing population and a declining number of people in the workforce (especially the full-time workforce), the balance of public/private fostering of citizen health, education, and welfare is tipped in favour of the corporate or private sector.

Part of the logic of capitalism is that the elements of maintenance and renewal and the attendant problems and social crises that capitalism precipitates must somehow be balanced. The welfare state was a particular response to this need. Teeple explains:

> Although sometimes used as a generic term for government intervention "on many fronts," the welfare state can also be seen as a capitalist *society* in which the state has intervened in the form of social policies, programs, standards, and regulations in order to mitigate class conflict and to provide for, answer, or accommodate certain social needs for which the capitalist mode of production in itself has no solution or provision. (Teeple, 2000: 15)

The **Keynesian Welfare State** (KWS)—the intervention of government into the business cycles of booms and busts—was a specific solution to problematic, capitalist-created by-products. As the welfare state is dismantled and atrophies, the private, domestic domain along with charities must pick up the slack. Included in this mix is the necessity for capital and the state to control the population. The social-control mechanisms within education are well documented (see, for example, Apple, 1979; Giroux, 1981; Bowles & Gintis, 1976). But an atrophying of human life, the moral or ethical dimension of the general good—citizen space—also takes place.

Who looks after the commons? (See Hardin, 1968.) Who cares for the needs of the common good? Who provides "care"? These costs will always be there; the transference from the public to the private in terms of responsibility becomes the transference from the public to the private sector of huge elements of created space for profitability.

Revitalizing Democracy, Regaining Public Space

To us, what appears to be at issue here is the fundamental nature of democratic life. To what systems of knowledge, information, and belief are we being socialized? How are our identities being created? Are our rights as citizens being restructured, or is it the economy that is undergoing a shift? Or both? Are the central issues that we as citizens should address being politicized or depoliticized? In effect, who is controlling this process? How are identities created within these contexts and contested realities?

It seems as though people who have just recently been enfranchised are being quickly disenfranchised as these processes continue. Just as groups move their power into public debate and discourse, they become further disadvantaged, further distanced from self-determination. For example, within the contemporary First Nations land claims questions, which public domain will be the site for social justice—the legal domain of the courts (application of some abstract rules) or the public, political process (negotiation within the domains of the state)? Who controls the public space? The private space? What role does ideology play as the basis of this control? What is the relationship between ideology and force or violence as forms of control? Where and how can we act in ways that reclaim this space?

Noam Chomsky (1999), among many others, is optimistic about the possibilities of public activism: he points out correctly that many of our past social gains were made possible through the participation of ordinary citizens. He contends that the rapid trend of global corporate control can be altered if ordinary citizens organize themselves to resist.

At issue here, is an understanding and definition of democracy. John Ralston Saul in his discussion of "The Good Citizen," notes, "Democracy isn't about decisiveness; it is about consideration. It is intended to be inefficient" (Saul, 1997b: 15). Democracy is based partly on intelligent conflict—educated citizens struggling to define the social and economic world in which they live. It necessarily involves a mixing and melding of diverse people, systems, and possibilities.

So why, if this is self-evident, isn't there a more effective defence—or even an offence—in favour of public service? Why is it when we mention Medicare, public corporations or public broadcasting, it is always with a romantic sound? "Ah, if only we could go back to the days when we had enough money." We fall into this kind of language, the language of the defeated, because we have accepted the basic language of corporatism. We have accepted language that delegitimizes the idea of the democratic state and the idea of the role of the citizen. There are various kinds of efficiency, and the least efficient organizations are the transnational corporations, because they are large managerial structures that have no

centre and no purpose and are frightened to think in the long term.
(Saul, 1997b: 15–16)

Implicit in Saul's comments are the embedded ideological phrases and caricatures of how the capitalist system works. To revitalize the citizen is to revitalize the public domain—the common social domain—with all its vagaries of accountability, responsibility, reliance, and interdependence. As it is now, ideological structures within society shape and delineate the nature of public space and, thus, public action. Out of the rubble of the ideological onslaught needs to surface a new citizen space— a space that reaches out and joins together the public/private divide.

CHAPTER 7

A Struggle for Identity and Greater Citizen Space

> My point is not that everything is bad, but that everything is danger-
> ous... (Foucault, quoted in Bailey & Gayle, 1993: 232)

> To awaken people to intelligent and articulate dissent, to give voice to
> their longings, to give both lease and license to their rage, to empower
> the powerless, to give voice to those who are enslaved by their own
> silence—certainly this represents a certain kind of danger. It is, indeed,
> the type of danger which a tortured society, but one that aspires in
> any way at all to human justice, ought to be eager to foster, search out
> and encourage. If this is a danger which our social system cannot possi-
> bly afford, then we are obliged to ask ourselves if we can possibly afford
> this social system. (Kozol, 1981: xv)

The concept of ideology, once given definition and example, becomes
a kind of enclosure, or determinant, of our lives. This enclosure is
mediated, constructed, and maintained by a range of ideologically encum-
bered institutions and structures. Even the clothing that covers our bodies
constitutes an enclosure driven by ideological contest and context. As
Fatima Mernissi's description of the *haik* (Chapter 1) reveals, the fabric of
our clothing is not just material; it has varied and problematic cultural
and ideological dimensions, which some would call "baggage." Indeed,
clothing in the broadest sense represents who we are; it helps mould our
identities. We may choose to live within the boundaries set by culture and
society, which may include living within the boundaries set by the state,

the media, or the corporate structures. We may be oblivious to these determinants, or we may be alert to their demands. We may be resistant to change or be advocates for greater social justice. But, however or wherever we are located within the complexities of contemporary society, we must recognize the demand for greater, more active **ideological literacy.** Only this will bring about greater social justice and more satisfying and equitable social relations.

To mobilize for democratic space, to take a greater citizen space, is of course no easy task. The complexity of the work demanded should be the catalyst to praxis—thoughtful, creative, intelligent action. Often, it seems, the stress placed on the postmodernist, fragmented identities of our time suggests a complexity that does not provide the space for concentrated, specific, sustained engagement. Still, the **sites of citizen space** created by an alertness to the ideological boundaries of our lives can become locations in which people can act and accomplish concrete, equitable goals within the context of authentic struggle, the space in which people can explore the dynamics of resistance and, possibly, rebellion.

Resistance versus Oppositional Behaviour

Particularly within educational theory (see Aronowitz & Giroux, 1983), the idea, or practice, of resistance has been counterpointed with **oppositional behaviour.** Resistance, within this frame, means thoughtful, intelligent, intentioned, critically alert action or praxis. This form of thought and action is activated by a careful reading of problematic situations or contexts; the resulting action of resistance has the potential to lead to a just outcome, such as the demands by local residents for the acquisition or return of parkland to their community for the enhancement of green space. The action may require an incredible amount of time, energy, and resources on the part of the voluntary community group as well as research and other resources from the municipality. The result, within the modern urban environment, may carry short- and long-term health advantages for both the community and the environment.

Oppositional behaviour refers to destructive, harmful behaviour—a flailing out at the system, a damaging form of action with outcomes that leave nothing, almost a form of nihilism or cynicism. This type of behaviour is often exemplified by "burning-down-the-school" forms of personal and property crimes or assaults. Characterized as destructive, it is distinct from resistance or recreation:

> Oppositional behavior may not be simply a reaction to powerlessness, but might be an expression of power fueled by and reproduc[ing] the most powerful grammar of domination ... For example, students may violate school rules, but the logic that informs such behavior may be rooted in forms of ideological hegemony such as racism and sexism. Moreover, the source of such hegemony often originates outside of the school. Under such circumstances, schools become social sites where oppositional behavior is simply played out, emerging less as a critique of schooling than as an expression of dominant ideology."
> (Aronowitz & Giroux, 1983: 100)

The building of ideologically literate communities demands that we allow a sense of resistance rather than various forms of oppositional behaviours to take hold of our imaginations. To speak about sites of citizen space is to suggest that it is possible to nurture creative human responses to problems within society, responses that are not distortions but examples of clarity. To recognize this possibility is also to comprehend the political nature of the continuum from resistance to oppositional behaviour. At times, for example, violence, although destructive, may expose demands for social change and exhibit fundamental social commitment on the part of individuals or groups within society. An uprising may be necessary to force some wished-for end, which will benefit the majority. All the sites on the continuum have their political and ideological moments. Even the expression "Whatever!" or the question "Who cares?" reflects a certain point, the point of apathy that those who, indeed, do care find worrisome.

It has become increasingly difficult, particularly given the influence of television, to distinguish between resistance, or resistant forms, and oppositional behaviours. Most television programs, for example, are driven by advertisements, which are, by their very definition, manipulative. In their most extreme form, people are urged metaphorically to kill for a pair of shoes or a leather jacket—and, indeed, people sometimes literally do just that. The world that Fatima Mernissi describes—that is, the world of Islam and its cultural demands—is aware of this and understands this from a different perspective. For young people in North America, peer pressure may be better characterized as market-driven peer pressure, the designer/brand name edition or obsession that has become known as "branding" (see Klein, 2000). One of the mythical ideological phrases of contemporary social life is the need or necessity of adolescent or teenage rebellion. How many teenagers are exploring creative authentic resistance, and how many are responding instead in a manner that can only be characterized as narcoleptic, influenced and sedated by designer/brand name fashion trends? How many acts are simply teenage oppositional behaviour that, in the end, leads only to continued oppression of the youth of our society?

Creating Citizen Space: A Sports Example

Constructed social boundaries, however created, can produce a multitude of cultural worlds or social environments. Understanding the genesis of these boundaries and the ideological formations that support various versions of them requires systematic investigation and examination. Schools and other social environments too often buy into whatever is the current representation of reality; indeed, they tend to support and nurture attitudes and behaviours that "go with the flow," in particular the brand/designer name edition or obsession.

The world of sports provides an example of the processes involved in this modern phenomenon. There are two ways of looking at or dealing with this world. Adopting a sports frame, for instance, means taking up the superstar world of Michael Jordan or Nike. A sporting frame (to change our view by language shift) represents a recognition of the wonder/awe, love, and respect for the game itself. Our attention here is focused on the constructed linguistic/behavioural space created within most sports sites, particularly with regard to the creation of adolescent, male identities. (See de Keseredy & Hinch, 1991, regarding how young men construct and maintain sexist, abusive behavioural patterns through their communications. See also, Burstyn, 1999 and Totten, 2000.)

Looking at the world of sport, Varda Burstyn (1999: 23) describes what she calls hyper-masculinity. Often, sports enthusiasts call this "character development" (see Burstyn, 1999: 43)—making men out of boys— for bell hooks, "men" reads "patriarchal, phallocentric, and masculine"(hooks, 1992: 87–88). Given the outcome, it might be called making boys out of boys. The concept of discipline, as it relates to sport or skill development in the arts, is informed by Michel Foucault's treatment and analysis of this term, as well as the work of Emile Durkheim. In Foucault's view (1979) discipline is control (social and personal) and a domain of study. Discipline moves between the creation and exercise of personal, social boundaries and the boundaries that are the fundamental discipline demands of, for example, good baseball as seen at the Canada Summer Games each year. From a coaching/teaching point of view, both of these boundaries need constant attention to detail or the outcome is sloppy sport played by boys on their way to becoming sexist, racist, homophobic "boys," that is, boys with no growth into, or recognition of, the complexities of modern social reality. Being a cool, athletic, sexy young male—if peer-driven and market-driven—can and often does mean utilizing offensive language (swear words heard on TV, or in movies, or on records, for instance) or homophobic epithets such as "fag." The treatment of women and women's lives, bodies, and spirits becomes a study in sexual objectification. Many sports enthusiasts say, "That's baseball!" or "Keep your PC crap to yourself—that's baseball"; or, as a baseball "mom" was heard to say, "Boys will be boys" (the justification for a good deal of male misbehaviour). Burstyn's interpretation of this sort of behaviour is interesting. Noting that "Today's erotic athletic flesh is hard, muscled, tense, and mean," she points out:

> Sport incites homoeroticism while it punishes homosexuality. The incited and frustrated homoerotic sexual energy of the sporting experience is one important source for the violence of men's sport. If we want to reduce the sources of violence in sport, we should address the fear of the feminine that underlies its violent homophobia. By forging

a physical culture in which the expressive and cooperative impulses are validated (as well as the assertive and instrumental), that fear could, at least in part, be attenuated, and its destructive consequences lessened. (Burstyn, 1999: 266–67)

The identities created do not in the end make for good athletes, particularly athletes who both respect and love the game. Identities, often constructed around obsessions about being "cool," seem to discourage the best from becoming the best they can possibly be. The notion that it was cool to smoke tobacco was invoked by cigarette companies in their fierce campaigns for new consumers in the early 1960s. Today, we have seen the dismal impact on people's health. Indeed, the term "cool" could use some thoughtful interrogation. Given the insights of Freire, Chomsky, and hooks (Chapter 4), we return to the notion of individual/community/corporate control of thought. Are there sites for citizen space—sites for critical learning and resistance to prepackaged, monolithic, "cool," social worlds? As sexualized, twentieth-century identities take hold within more and more social sites, these sites slowly lose their capacity to act outside of a sexualized framework. In other words, as more and more aspects of everyday life become sexualized, our degree of freedom to learn and participate in social experience (without expressing sexualized identities) becomes diminished (see Foucault, 1980: 219–20).

The boys are trying so hard to become cool that they have lost their opportunity, at least for the moment, of becoming real people or, in this case, effective athletes. If the boundaries regarding sexist, racist, and homophobic behaviours—to say nothing of other ideologically ingested information and ideologically bought clothing—had been established differently, much of what plays out as 16- to 18-year-olds acting like four-year-olds in a sandbox might give way to better quality sport as well as better quality character and community development. All this concerns the creation and maintenance of a proper citizen space. Boys could grow into men who have greater respect for sport and an understanding of the diversity of community within which they will participate as adults, if they are not seduced by fashion into behaviour that is "cool." To just cite two examples, this diversity is expressed by the diversity of a multicultural society with a multiplicity of sexual expressions. Amazingly, all levels of public schooling, especially secondary schools, have turned a blind eye to some of the most significant experiences of youth on the street, in the sports arena, from the media, from their music. Insight into popular culture and an understanding of cultural criticism could be a mainstay of secondary curriculum, but often the opposite is the case; that is, consumer-created realties prevail.

As it is, internalized ideology controls, influences, or shapes identity formation both in substance and process. Individuals, but youth in particular, need domains or spaces that foster a critical, alert analysis of the ideological enclosures within which their lives are played out. Sixteen- to 18-year-old young men who want to become as good as they possibly can at the game of baseball, for example, need to build the game, to renew it, within a context that allows them to focus on the discipline of baseball, not on their ability to be cool, or sexualized. The same point can be made of the worlds of dancers, musicians, artists, actors, or even ordinary citizens.

In *Darwin's Athletes*, John Hoberman (1997) focuses on our society's infatuation with African American athletic achievement and the eventual athleticizing of African American identity (see also, Spence, 1999). Hoberman makes the compelling argument that this infatuation, which expresses itself through media representations, the sports industry, athletes, and spectators, has played a destructive role in the lives of African Americans and a disturbing role in race relations. Conferring a more or less god-like status onto the most popular African American athletes, he argues, tends to blur the existence of racial inequality in society, with significant implications. When White boys construct their sports identities within the framework of being cool, the practice often serves to discourage them from being the best they can possibly be. But when young White boys do not become sports superstars, they usually still have many other options open to them. The situation is different for young African American boys in the sense that "the sports fixation damages Black children by discouraging academic achievement in favour of physical self-expression, which is widely considered a racial trait" (Hoberman, 1997: 8). The preoccupation with sports superstardom and the rejection of academic achievement among young African Americans help to close an already small door to other options. Along with the athleticizing of African American identity is the associated notion that African Americans are capable only of utilizing their bodies and not their minds. When sportscasters or sports writers articulate athletic attributes, they usually focus on muscle power rather than mental adroitness or mental determination. African American children internalize these attributes; indeed, many of them taunt their peers who show interest in academic fields. When asked about societal role models, many of the children respond by citing sports stars, but statistically not many of them will be able to achieve success on that level. Hoberman emphasizes:

> Sports themes and styles have soaked into the fabric of African American life, as black identity is athleticized through ubiquitous role models who stimulate wildly unrealistic ambitions in black children (an improbable number of black boys expect to become professional athletes) and initiate athletic fashion trends and hairstyles. In short, it has become all too easy for many blacks and whites to assume that the horizons of black life are co-terminus with the achievements of athletes, and one of the most damaging and least publicized corollaries of the sports obsession has been a pronounced rejection of intellectual ambition. (Hoberman, 1997: 4)

As of yet no significant campaign has been mounted by leaders in African American communities to stem the tide of African American athleticism (as a commonly held goal) and attitudes of anti-intellectualism. As bell hooks (1992: 89) notes:

> There has never been a time in the history of the United States when black folks, particularly black men, have not been enraged by the dominant culture's stereotypical, fantastical representation of black masculinity. Unfortunately, black people have not systematically challenged these narrow visions, insisting on a more accurate "reading" of black male reality. Acting in complicity with the *status quo*, many black people have passively absorbed narrow representations of black masculinity, perpetuated stereotypes, myths, and offered one-dimensional accounts.

Contemporary black men have been shaped by these representations. (hooks, 1992: 89)

In this task of exploring possible citizen spaces—the contemporary behavioural and linguistic enclosures that shape responses to ideological matters—another element is how modern corporate nation-state relationships are worked out legally, especially within various trade and other international agreements. In contrast to the personal and political movement level of identity politics, another level altogether—that of law and major trade agreements (present or forthcoming)—have established the identity of corporations as "persons" and "citizens" under the law. The language and the law meld to forge new identities at levels within the society never before conceived. Clarke states:

> Corporations, unlike human beings, can potentially live forever. They can exist in many places at once. They can alter their identities and become different "persons." They can sell themselves to new owners. Above all, corporations possess economic and political resources which citizens, for the most part, could never hope to accumulate. (Clarke, 1997: 111)

In this context—of rights given and taken, and with the illusive attraction of the larger game being played so dominantly by the iconic likes of sports superstars and others— the opportunities for becoming full citizens are limited, especially for young people. As Clarke notes:

> Not only have "citizen rights" in a democratic society been superseded by "investor rights" in the new global economy, the very role and meaning of the term "citizen" [have] been changed and distorted. Concerted campaigns waged by the Fraser Institute and the Reform Party have, in effect, reduced the role of "citizens" to that of "taxpayers" and "consumers" in our political culture. (Clarke, 1997: 145)

The highly touted lean production of the time has slowly developed a lean citizen: "The *lean citizen*: one whose allegiances are no longer to some broader collective but to a diversity of 'communities of consumption' and lifestyle, or to moral, religious or ethnic communities" (Mooers, 1998: 46). These "communities of consumption" reflect the values of the brand/designer-name edition obsession.

But if the domain of the consumer is filled with illusions and ideologically driven enclosures, the workplaces of young people are no less afflicted. Youth, often that group with the most disposable income at hand, become addicted consumers who consume the "stuff" proffered by contemporary society. On the shop floor, this same group often become cynical, alert to the exploitation, oppression, and lack of quality and creativity in the workplace. Their identities are nurtured as consumers, but are manipulated as employees.

Sites of Citizen Space

As the world becomes more economically, socially, and politically globalized, more knowledge-based, and more technologically advanced, resistance to dominant representations becomes more and more necessary. Partly, this resistance means returning to our sites of ease and comfort—"the comfort zones," sites of struggle, and sites of community—which also means attempting to place or locate conceptually public and private moments as they unfold around us.

Throughout each day we make decisions and choices, expend energy, and cast laboured dollars into the variety of communities within which we move and live. Many people feel either powerless in the face of the globalized social, economic, and political realities that touch them—massaging and mauling them—or they feel diminished in relationship to much that surrounds them (for example, by mergers of global corporations that can alter their lives in a variety of ways). But how do we fight the placing of cola machines in a high-school auditorium? We need to unpack and unwrap the process within the context of twenty-first-century educational structures with a recognition of the masking and hiding that has taken place within education itself. The flywheel of consumerism continues to turn, particularly as the school encounters corporate demands and funding realities.

If we are to move into a more democratic form of social relations and social structure, we need to recognize again the need for sites of citizen space. The interplay between the individual and the society becomes more complex as it is filled with externally determined mechanisms of control—ideological formations that direct or influence our daily lives. It doesn't help in this regard, we believe, to be overly deterministic, a position suggesting that human beings are enclosed in a straitjacket, with all our moves tightly restricted, far beyond any personal, individual control or application of imagination. Rather, we believe in the desire for greater human freedom within a collectivity or community that is more justly democratic. Therefore, we want to recognize and admire courageous human responses to the often oppressive circumstances in which we live and work.

In his book *One-Dimensional Man* (a title that seems more apt as the feminist perspective continues its cultural critique), Herbert Marcuse describes what he calls "the happy consciousness… the belief that the real is rational and that the system delivers the goods—reflects the new conformism which is a facet of technological rationality translated into social behavior" (Marcuse, 1964: 84). We have used the term "narcosis" with similar meaning and intent—that there is an incipient passivity— what Marcuse later calls "pacified existence" (Marcuse, 1964: 235). Certainly, "happy consciousness" or the mindset or behaviour of the individual who sleepwalks through the everyday world is a conspicuous element in today's society—both in representational forms and reality. For example, many of Hollywood's so-called comedies present individuals who appear to be stunned by modern life. Our educational systems and other conduits of information and conceptual knowledge often appear to be sites laden with trivialized response rather than courageous action. Herbert Schiller's *The Mind Managers* discusses the unacknowledged cultural impact of the recreation and entertainment industries:

> Though all the myths on which mind management depends are found in the recreational-entertainment products of the Madison Avenue-Hollywood word-and-image factories, one central myth dominates the world of fabricated fantasy; the idea that entertainment and recreation

are value-free, have no point of view, and exist outside, so to speak, the social process.

An enormously diverse consciousness-processing apparatus, utilizing all the familiar forms of popular culture—comic books, animated cartoons, movies, TV and radio shows, sports events, newspapers and magazines—takes full advantage of this totally false conception. The communications industry pumps out value-laden recreation and entertainment, denying all the while any impact beyond momentary escapism and a happy state of relaxation. (Schiller, 1973: 79–80)

While many people are indeed victimized, fearful, distracted workaholics, there are others who are community activists, genuinely hopeful and critically acute to the events in their daily lives. We observe many whose courage is defined and exhibited daily within contexts filled with violence and destruction as well as those who do not get the air-time of the celebrity but who are applying powerful remedies to the complexities and problems of daily life. From "happy consciousness" to "critical consciousness" is a long journey. It can also be a collective experience, one undertaken by many with the optimism that the result will be just and uplifting.

Towards Some Basic Principles

To come to any real understanding of ideology and how it works in society, to come to grips with it, and to move on: all of this demands that we become critics of our society, changing our participation and perception within that society. Here we would like to suggest seven principles that we think typify this change or shift in thinking about how we live, work, and act within the contemporary complexities of society.

1. *Acquire ideological literacy.* If we are to become literate about the ideological influences that surround us, we need to be alert to the language, images, representations, and everyday ways in which we can read the world(s) we inhabit. As with any form of literacy, this project demands study; it will not emerge full-blown in our consciousness.
2. *Claim greater citizen space.* To gain ideological literacy means that we

act, live, and study within real contexts in spaces that we come to know as we begin to comprehend the ways in which they shape our lives. To be citizens within these spaces demands that we recognize our entitlement as active co-producers of our circumstances, rather than perceiving our part in both public and private domains as owned and operated by those with advantage and power.

3. *Promote resistance and re-creation.* To be activists, we must energize our actions by finding the limits of the present space conceptually as well as in concrete forms. To resist is to become fortified with "street" power—citizen power. Everyone must resist national and international attempts to displace the citizen from moments of historic significance. Witness the demonstrations and reactions by the authorities to them that have occurred during such meetings as the World Trade Organization, Seattle, 1999; the World Bank and International Monetary Fund, Washington, 2000; the Organization of American States, Windsor, Ontario, 2000; the World Petroleum Congress, Calgary, 2000; the Summit of the Americas, Quebec City, 2001; and the G8 Summit, Kananaskis, Alberta, 2002. We must also resist the emergent "fortress society"—that is, the gated, security-driven, affluent community, as Jeremy Rifkin (1995) calls it—the mindset that would close borders and refuse international aid or cooperation. The ideological contests are enormous within these frameworks of globalized transnational action. The resisters, more often than not, are also alert to ways of recreating these processes and the ways they are represented to us.

4. *Overcome privileged narcosis.* We need to awaken to and thoroughly comprehend the historical and crosscultural dynamics of life. To emerge out of the events of September 11, 2001, without awakening to the great power differentials within world politics and the need for significant redistribution of resources and opportunities would be to fall asleep once again. Privilege tends to blind us to the impoverished material reality that faces most of the world's population. Obviously, not all people are privileged. All of us have work to do on this score; we are all implicated in the imbalances, injustices, and, indeed, the horrors of the past two centuries.

5. *Act in diverse and creative ways.* Both creativity and diversity can easily be overlooked or closed off in the domains of thought and action. To live within diverse communities and act in creative ways demand courage and imagination. To begin to live in ways that foster these elements of being human, we must present to children very early on the ways in which these can be lost by prepackaged forms of representation, humour, and controlled imagination. Learning the brands must mean learning the foreground and background out of which these emerge.

6. *Identify the boundaries.* Who pays, who profits, who controls, who cares, who is victimized? Such questions must form the basis of our critical analysis. To identify the boundaries is to live an alert, compellingly alive existence. Increasingly, the "Who am I?" question needs to be broadened to "Where am I?" The limits of our lives are just as crucial to our survival as are our potentialities or possibilities.

7. *End youth workplace/consumerplace exploitation.* If we broaden the sites of work to sites of study for youth and examine this greater complex within the ways we acquire what we need to live full, creative lives, we must reinvent communities that are inclusive of youth in ways that recognize their place as citizens. To see youth as a market, both for labour and profitable consumer dollars, is to deny us all the right to live in societies that are more than economic tombs. To recreate citizenship means moving beyond exploitation. At this juncture in history, youth inhabit one of the sites of greatest exploitation.

Take a five-minute walk through the dynamics of our daily life; take a five-minute segment of television that includes one commercial; take a five-minute section of a college/university class in any subject; take a five-minute commute (by foot, cycle, car, train, or ferry); take a five-minute read of the newspaper's front page; take a five-minute lunch (at home or away from home); take five minutes of time with someone you care a good deal about. Afterwards, run each of these seven principles through that five minutes. They are not a checklist, but are intended as questions for a process of awakening out of narcosis—out of a society in which the boundaries seem always to be set elsewhere.

John Ralston Saul commenting on the "anti-intellectualism of false populists," notes, "What frightens ideologues about culture is that it is uncontrollable. ... Referenda, false populism, ideology are all about control" (Saul, 1997a: 263). It seems tragically comical that, at the beginning of a new century and millennium filled already with social injustice, wars around the globe, a widening gap in the distribution of wealth, disparities in educational resources, and so on, one of our most common, somewhat mechanical responses to almost everything is "no problem" or "no worries." To call this narcosis "denial" seems almost hackneyed. Yet, to climb out of the ideological enclosure is certainly a demanding undertaking. What is this flywheel that continues to turn? Its heavy momentum is not going to dissipate. Our project is to identify for each other the masks that are descending to obscure our vision. Then we can begin to see sites for citizen space and act within democratic worlds. The words of writer Susan Griffin might help in this endeavour. She urges us to comprehend our own experiences of ideological moments and structures:

> Ideology. Ideology, form and dialogue. One begins as a socialist arguing that matter comes before spirit. One wins a revolution and vanquishes the enemy. But then one discovers the enemy is not yet dead. She is a poet whose words are vaguely unsettling. Who doubts. And then there are the prisons again, the police again, the old terror again. The war is still waging.
>
> And there is still a war waging within me. I have been schooled in the ways of this culture. In my own mind unknowingly I choose the same solution to emotional dilemma that my culture has chosen and has taught me to choose. Though I argue against pornography and racism, my own mind splits against itself, creates a "you." Now this "you" is the ideologist, a part of myself I hide from myself. She is afraid of my own creativity. She asks old questions which exclude the possibility of new insights. She has categorical ideas of thought or expression from which she will not deviate. She dismisses my ideas with labels, epithets, catch phrases. She purposely misinterprets me and seizes on small mistakes to humiliate me.
>
> And she is a martinet. She wants to produce a comprehensive world

view so that nothing in the world is unexplained. She is a Prussian soldier in the world of intellect. She is not interested in unanswered questions, in uncertainties, intuitions, barely grasped insights, hunches. Moreover she wishes every idea to be consistent, to conform to one ideal. (Griffin 1982: 646–47)

Griffin calls on us to examine the difficulties that inevitably arise as we look to social change. Her articulation of her own struggle can help us all to engage with, and enter, the problematic of resistance.

Glossary

acculturation: The act of adapting to or adopting a different culture or cultural perspective. When two cultures come in contact with one another, one cultural group may adopt the language, values, and cultural traits of the other, or they may both adopt characteristics of the other. This adoption of new cultural traits may be between cultures or generations. See **socialization**.

achieved status: Social position that one acquires as a result of one's talents, abilities or merits or lack thereof. This is the basis of meritocracy, i.e. that society's resources or status positions are awarded on the basis of achievement, not on the basis of favouritism etc. See **ascribed status**.

affirmative action: First implemented in the United States, policies and programs that are designed to create opportunities for groups that have been disadvantaged historically. These policies and programs, usually instituted within the workplace and the educational system, are an attempt to reverse historical discrimination. See **employment equity**.

ascribed status: Refers to the social position in which one is born. This often includes aspects of one's identity which are not changeable or not easily changeable, for example, one's ethnic/racial identity or one's sex. See **achieved status**.

Asia Pacific Economic Conference (APEC): Represents a free-trade initiative consisting of 18 member countries. It began as a Pacific regional forum for economic co-operation but quickly moved towards a strong commitment to trade and investment liberalization. Its focus is on market-driven activities, deregulation, privatization, nominal controls on resource exploitation, and unrestricted foreign investments. Member countries include Australia, Brunei, Canada, Chile, China, Hong Kong, Indonesia, Japan,

Malaysia, Mexico, New Zealand, Papua New Guinea, the Philippines, Singapore, South Korea, Taiwan, Thailand, and the United States. The 1997 APEC meetings in Vancouver were marked by street protests mostly in opposition to the politics of Indonesia's President Suharto.

carriers of culture: Perhaps best defined by example: advertisements, whether on TV or other media, utilize sites or dynamics within a culture that sustain or maintain the taken-for-granted, shared ways of doing things. Beer commercials feature young people having fun, at leisure, and typify the dress, cars, and furniture that have cultural legitimacy and, to some extent, cultural predictability.

citizen: An individual who is a voting member of a **nation-state**. Citizenship is a right that may be acquired through naturalization. The concept of the citizen and the power that citizenship affords individuals within particular nations are not only diverse in nature but very much contested, since they deal with fundamental rights such as freedom of speech, expression, and assembly.

citizen space: Within the context of the thesis of this book, sites of citizen space refer to those locations, places, and moments of action and hope that provide people with points of departure and resistance to increase the dynamics of social justice within their lives in society.

civil society: Within the **nation-state**, the domain that lies between the **state** and the personal, private, domestic relationships of people. It is the domain of life that characterizes community and neighbourhood experience as well as the working economic lives outside the home for most people.

commodification: When objects are given **exchange value**, they become commodities in the exchange systems or market systems within societies. To commodify is to give a particular object marketable value. In a sociological sense, it is the process by which aspects of culture become marketable items. Commodification can also be perceived as a process of objectification or dehumanization – making a commodity of human beings. See **reification**.

conflict theory: A perspective of society that focuses on macro-level structures, such as the dynamics of social classes, etc. It emphasizes the struggle between advantaged and disadvantaged groups, one attempting to maintain their advantage, the other to increase theirs. The theoretical perspectives of Karl Marx and Max Weber are most often associated with conflict theory. See **dialectical materialism**.

consensus theory: Typified by the work of Emile Durkheim, consensus theory assumes that the social dynamics of a particular society are the result of a consensus or agreement among the people of that society. Often this perspective, which presumes social cohesion, is based on the interdependencies characteristic of differentiated institutions.

conservatism: (Note: lower case "c" denotes political/philosophical perspective or position rather than reference to a specific political party.) That part of the political spectrum that believes in maintaining the existing order or the status quo, **ascribed status**, economic privilege, and a higher authority within society than the individual (most commonly religious), which, therefore, gives rise to a dynamic, "organic", tension between community and individual. See distinction with **neo-conservatism, neo-liberalism, liberalism**, and **socialism**. See also, Chapter 1.

conspiracy theory: A perspective or theory that attributes to social events or sites of social advantage the suggestion that these have been established by a group of people working together (conspiring = breathing together) to gain power and advantage for themselves over others, usually by manipulative, surreptitious, or devious means. See distinction with **structural analysis** or **self-interest analysis**.

contextualization: To place an idea or concept both within real context or social, historical circumstances and within a framework where meaning may be clarified, illustrated, or more precisely ascertained.

corporatization: The movement to globalized economic power by transnational corporations, often with the blessing of the state or enabling legislation from the state, leading to the take-over of everyday practices by corporate demands and ideologies. Our everyday language is being transformed by this process: the student becomes a consumer/client of education, the patient also becomes a consumer/client of medical goods and services. The process is reinforced by an abundance of corporate advertising.

defective individualism: Assumes that individual success or failure is the result of individual effort, achievement, or talent. If one fails, it is because of some individual, defective attribute. (The counterpoint to **faulty structure** as described by Bolaria, 1995.)

democracy: Governance by the **citizens** of a political community or **nation-state**. Democracy, contrary to popular belief, is based in authentic conflict— that one or all can engage in conflicting debates and viewpoints without direct threat of death or violence. It is government "for the people, by the people", ... Democratic actions assume some social justice and equity, as well as recognition of rights such as freedom of speech, expression, and assembly.

democratic socialism: Socialism that is typified by democratic relationships and structures. Within the political spectrum democratic socialism is perceived as being more to the left or more socialist than is **social democracy**. This perspective allows the private ownership of some of the means of production, government distribution of goods and services, and open elections.

de-politicization (to de-politicize): To remove from public political discussion, to attempt to neutralize something that is overtly political in nature. Often this process means taking something out of a contested domain and making it appear to be neutral, hiding or obscuring its political dimensions. **Medicalization** is an example of this; that which had a history of being within the community is re-located within the domain of experts, in this case physicians and other health care professionals. See Chapter 3.

deregulation: Removal from state jurisdiction aspects of the state apparatus that have traditionally been sites of state oversight; systematically downsizing government regulation. Deregulation is part of the agenda of **neo-liberalism**, as is **privatization.**

dialectics: Involves recognition of the conflicting, contradictory perspectives and realities that make up social worlds; a two-way, interactive relationship rather than a one-way determinism. For example, Georg Friederich Hegel, the nineteenth-century German philosopher, argued that history is the history of ideas; i.e., a thesis is forwarded, an anti-thesis conflicts with it, resulting in a new synthesis which becomes a new thesis, and so on. The dialectical method of Marx suggested that the basis of historical movement is located in the contradictions of the material world (i.e., **dialectical materialism**).

dialectical materialism: A perspective of history grounded in the view that social change is the result of conflicting, contradictory forces within the lived, everyday economic realities of people. Within the study of dialectics, Marx's dialectical materialism is opposed to the **idealism** of Hegel, which presupposes that ideas are the movers of history. See **historical materialism.**

discourse: The talk, words, concepts, ideas, practices, and arrangements contained within a particular discipline or group and its language formations; for example, the discourse of sociology, medicine or the discourse on modern sexuality. For Foucault, that which can, and cannot, be said about something. The term "jargon" is often associated with the contained discourse of specific groups.

employment equity: Basically, hiring practices that are intended to match the social make-up of the population within which a particular job is advertised. Often mistakenly perceived as a quota system, employment equity attempts to hire members of historically disadvantaged groups such as **White** women, First Nations peoples, people of colour, and people with disabilities. See **affirmative action**.

epistemology: A set of assumptions about the nature of knowledge; the study or theory of knowledge and how we come to know what we do know.

essentialism: Assumes categories of thought regarding a phenomenon which exists prior to our apprehension of the phenomenon itself (an idealist perspective). These essences or ideal forms, because of their pre-existing nature, shape or form people's perceptions and often become the basis of stereotypes. Recently, this concept, especially the notion of biology as central to explanations of gender and sex differences, has come under attack, particularly by feminist social theorists. See **social constructivism**.

etymology: The genesis or origin of words both in form and sense.

exchange value: The value of a commodity in the marketplace, based on its economic relationship to other commodities. See **use value** and **sign value**.

false consciousness: A concept from Marx's theory that examines the capacity of a group or class to deny its apparent social/political/economic self-interest. Occasionally this concept is related to Jean Paul Sartre's notion of self-deception. This term has profound relevance for the study of ideology, mystification, and representation or mis-representation, as well as of revolutionary consciousness and action.

faulty structure (related to **defective individualism**): Bolaria's exploration of the need for a structural analysis of social problems and issues. Rather than blaming the victim, Bolaria suggests the need for a sound structural perspective; for example, regarding the reasons for poverty.

feminism: A theoretical perspective that advocates human equality, social justice and the profound understanding of the standpoint of women, to use Dorothy Smith's term, (1987: 106–07) within the complex social structures of society. A movement towards the elimination of women's oppression and to greater equal rights, it also focuses on putting mechanisms in place to ensure that these rights are maintained.

feminist epistemology: Acquiring knowledge from the standpoint of women, that is, being cognizant of the socio-historical context from which individuals emerge and exist; the call for a women's theory of knowledge and advocacy for a feminist comprehension of the production, reproduction, and dissemination of knowledge in society. (See Smith, 1987: 17–18.)

free market: The political/economic doctrine that advocates that the state stay clear of the market (the "invisible hand," according to Adam Smith) to allow the enterprising efforts of business to function unhindered. It is a mythical perspective, or mystifying, in that its so-called desire for purity seems to cloud the reality of economic relationships in contemporary societies. See **neo-conservatism/neo-liberalism**.

generalized other: George Herbert Mead's term referring to the values and meanings of the wider social community to which an individual becomes socialized and within which the individual develops a sense of self-identity. See **significant other**.

globalization: The significant shift in the later half of the twentieth century to world economies, world ideologies, and world cultural/consumer realities that dominate and envelop national/regional/local worlds; i.e., interdependent, interlocked trans-global economies. The globalized world of transnational corporations (TNCs) transcends the power of **nation-states** and transforms the social/political/economic realities that people experience in their everyday lives and communities. See Chapter 4, p. 116, for a more detailed definition.

hegemony (or **ideological hegemony**; Gramsci, 1971): The ideological domination of the ruling class over the subordinate classes. This is accomplished and maintained as the dominant ideas are presented as the only reasonable ones, particularly in ideological institutions such as the media and the educational system. Alternative ideas are usually not considered.

historical materialism: Refers to Marx's perspective that the trajectory of history is that of material/economic relationships and realities (how people meet their basic needs). In essence, the analysis of social life should begin with the predominant modes of production and the social relations that these generate rather than with the **idealist perspective** of Hegel, the eighteenth-century German philosopher. See **dialectical materialism** and **materialism**.

idealism or **idealist perspective/position:** The perspective that essences exist or that ideas are the foundation of reality. In Georg Friedrich Hegel's work —countered by Feuerbach, then Marx, with the materialist perspective—

this posits that the trajectory of history is the **dialectical** struggle of ideas. See **materialism**.

identity: A number of complex meanings arise here. First of all, identity can mean likeness with something, or sameness. However, identity as used here is the sense of self that emerges out of the complexities of the socialization process. The two definitions become problematic when we recognize the potential for an individual to have multiple or fragmented identities in post-modern society. An individual may experience a multiplicity of identities constituted through race/ethnicity, gender, sexual orientation, culture, etc.

identity politics: Emerged as a response to challenges by groups of working-class women, lesbians, and women of colour to the assumption of "universal woman." It assumes that cultural, racial/ethnic, and sexual identities are diverse and that the presentation of identity in social life should be determined by those within particular groups, rather than by media representation or some other outside entity. The concept of identity politics is endemic to post-modern societies and is the major focus of **feminism** and **multiculturalism**.

ideological domination: Closely related to **ideological hegemony**, it refers to the control and overall dominance of a particular ideology within a socio-cultural system or society.

ideological hegemony: See **hegemony**.

ideological literacy: In some sense the negation or the absence of **false consciousness**. Ideological literacy refers to a clarity of perception regarding the ideological forces at play in society. It assumes critical consciousness regarding social/cultural/environmental/political realities.

ideology: As noted in Chapter 1, a brief definition might be: "A set of beliefs that seem to serve and shape the interests of a certain group in society, has a legitimating/justifying function, and has the power to control or influence how people think about, or act in, their social circumstances." Fundamentally, ideas that help us to make sense of our everyday world, although such ideas can oftentimes obscure certain contradictions in society, such as social inequality, and can help to maintain the status quo. See Chapter 2 for a variety of definitions regarding this term.

ideology of individualism: Refers to the perspective that one wins or loses in life's competitive struggles on the basis of one's own skills, abilities, and advantages. If one wins, the rewards will be in various forms that will justify the individual nature of the success, i.e., property, wealth, prestige, etc. See

meritocracy and **social Darwinism**. Also, see Joe Feagin's definition in Chapter 4.

instrumental rationality: Often counterpointed with affective or expressive perspectives, this refers to logical, reasoned, measurable, predictable, efficiency-based domains of rational behaviour; the ability to get things done, for example, building a bridge.

intentionality: The term used by Husserl, Schutz, and other phenomenologists to recognize that consciousness is always "consciousness of .... something." One intends what he or she will be aware of.

interactionism: A sociological school of thought called Symbolic Interactionism, a term coined by Herbert Blumer, to refer to those micro-theorists (e.g., Charles Horton Cooley and George Herbert Mead) who focus on the interactions among people, particularly with regard to symbolic formations, especially language and gesture. Social meanings arise out of interaction.

Keynesian Welfare State (KWS): Named for its theorist, British economist John Maynard Keynes (1883–1946), this refers to the intervention by the state in the cyclical nature of the economy to prevent extreme downturns. By holding surpluses created during good economic times and utilizing these in bad times, the state can boost a flagging economy.

laissez-faire capitalism: See **free market**.

liberalism: (Note: lower case "l" denotes political/philosophical perspective or position rather than reference to a specific political party). The centrist position on the political spectrum, a perspective that advocates individualism, freedom, reasoned rationality, the scientific method, and meritocracy. See distinction with **neo-conservatism, neo-liberalism, conservatism, socialism.**

legitimacy: To give public credibility and currency to ideas, people, objects, icons, etc. Often legitimacy refers to that which is established within the status quo arrangements of society.

macro-theory: The domain of sociology that studies the larger picture, the overarching institutional structures of society. See **micro-theory**.

masculinity: A socially constructed view of what males in a particular society should be, i.e., manliness. Obviously, a multiplicity of possibilities are available. Note, Varda Burstyn's expression "hypermasculinity" referring to sports and athletic views of what maleness should be not only in sport but in social life in general (Burstyn, 1999).

materialism: Originally forwarded by Feuerbach, then by Marx, in counter-distinction to **idealism,** materialism refers to the exploration of the economic, material realities that people face in their everyday lives and recognizes that these realities are the forces with power to determine how we live. Feuerbach notes, "We must eat before we philosophize."

medicalization: The appropriation of more and more domains of social life by the medical community; generally, a form of social control that increasingly puts the power in the hands of "experts." Social problems that once were outside the domain of professional or institutionalized services begin to come under their control. See **de-politicization.**

meritocracy: A hierarchical social system in which the structuring and distribution of rewards are based on skill, merit, and ability or certification of these; problematic in societies with unequal access to resources. Characterized by the phrase, "It's not who you know, but what you know" or its more common obverse.

micro-theory: The domain of social theory that deals with the experience of individual, small groups or the face-to-face interactions of people in their everyday lives; opposed to **macro-theory,** which explores the "big picture" issues of social structure.

multiculturalism: In Canada, one of the main sites of the origin of this term, multiculturalism refers first to policy (1971), then to law (1988) in which the complexities of diverse immigration patterns have created a multicultural, multi-ethnic social reality, i.e., cultural pluralism. It has been explored in social scientific literature and research as an ideology, a policy, a law, and a verifiable social reality. Its main objective is the harmonious co-existence of different cultural or ethnic groups.

narcosis: Literal meaning is the desire to go to sleep, or induced stupor, or insensibility. It is used within this book as a metaphor regarding our inability to see clearly the social realities that face us daily, due to ideological masking. A state of being unaware, or unconscious of one's political, economic, and social environment. As used here, it is related to **false consciousness.**

nationalism: Patriotism; reverence and affinity to one's nation and the process of nation-building. In extreme form, a dangerously ideological force that affirms violence as legitimate action for social change and fosters ethno-centric, jingoistic, and racist perspectives.

nation-state: Originating in the seventeenth and eighteenth centuries, the nation-state is the modern organization of governance within boundaried political, economic, and socio-cultural territories. Its development over the past centuries has been seen as not only inevitable, but also as the legitimate domain of political control. Today, it has been suggested that **globalization** will lead to its demise or that, at least, the power of nation-states will be superseded or curtailed by the power of **transnational corporations** (TNCs). **Nationalism** is a complex ideological outcome of the nation-state.

neo-conservatism: that position on the political spectrum to the right of liberalism, better characterized as **neo-liberalism,** below.

neo-liberalism: Formerly, called neo-conservatism (the emergent New Right or the Radical Right), neo-liberalism is the political perspective that advocates **deregulation, privatization,** and tax cuts. Its emphasis is on individual freedom (particularly from government or other people in general) it emerges out of a **social Darwinist,** "survival of the fittest" perspective, originally forwarded by Herbert Spencer. This particular ideology has currency in contemporary society.

oppositional behaviour: A term that has risen within educational theory in counterdistinction to **resistance.** Oppositional behaviour is seen as destructive lashing out at the system or establishment on the part of individuals who have no analysis or comprehension of the forces that may be oppressing them.

Otherness: A term that demands recognition of "the Other", regardless of differences in sex, sexual orientation, race or ethnicity, or social class. This Otherness usually serves as a basis for legitimizing exclusion, subordination, or exploitation. Race, gender, and class differences play a significant role in its social construction. In cultural and post-colonial studies, emphasis is placed on the examination of how Others are represented. See Chapter 5.

pedagogy: The study and theory of education; the overall teaching/learning experience; the practice of teaching. In a specific sense, educators such as Henry Giroux and Paulo Freire have argued for a radical pedagogical practice wherein pedagogy is not separate from politics; it consists of a form of cultural politics within classrooms. For these educators, pedagogy must include a form of critical literacy that places at its centre society's unequal relations.

people of colour: A problematic term because of its referent point being people's skin colour, used both commonly and within the social sciences in counterdistiction to being "White."

political correctness: A term that emerged in the 1990s, particularly at many

North American campuses, as an antagonistic reference to the language and action of those advocating social justice within society. The work of those advocating social justice was based on the assumption that North American educational institutions were Eurocentric, racist, and sexist and that involvement in antiracist/antisexist struggles was necessary to reverse this. This reversal could be accomplished by a more diverse curriculum. Neo-conservative groups (later called neo-liberals) who, with the help of conservative think-tanks, launched a campaign against these programs, called these efforts at social justice, "political correctness" or "PC." Today, the expression has taken on a moral, everyday usage, which suggests that if one ascribes to politically correct language or actions, one is somehow trying to protect social justice or egalitarian initiatives, i.e., programs that from a neo-liberal perspective should be "liberated" from such "false protections."

politicize: To give political meaning or to recognize the publicly contested nature of a particular event or idea; also, to move an experience or idea from private to public domain, thereby laying it open to public debate. See **depoliticization** and Chapter 4.

postmodernism: A term for contemporary social reality that emerged from art and architecture to herald the transcendence of established modern forms, then was extended to forms of authority, legitimacy, rationality, etc., in a more general social sense. Related to post-structuralism, postmodernism characterizes a society that is fragmented, with a multiplicity of identities, in which the canon of science and other forms of legitimacy and authority are open to question.

praxis: Refers to the unity of thought, word, action, and reflection to promote social/political/ economic change.

public/private divide: Recognition of the emergent, significant, and complex separation of the public and private domains of human experience.

privatization: Refers to the removal, sale, or transfer of nationalized Crown corporations, such as Air Canada, Canadian National Railways, and Petro-Canada from the public sector to privately-owned companies or corporations. Ideologically, the process of privatization tends to diminish the credibility of the public sector or the public domain to provide goods and services. See **neo-liberalism, neo-conservatism**.

racialization: An action, behaviour, or presentation of ideas that makes race or ethnicity central. It refers to a political and ideological process by which particular groups are identified by direct or indirect reference to their real or imagined phenotype, which essentializes the group solely as a biological unit. Racialization may not in itself be racist, yet it clearly situates the concept of race and ethnicity within a particular social domain or **discourse**. See Chapter 5.

racism: A form of prejudice and/or discrimination based on physical characteristics, such as skin colour, hair type, eye configuration, or other dynamics of ethnic origin such as religion, nationality, or language. Racism can be expressed in a variety of ways.

reification: Often referred to as "thingizing," reification is an act of forgetting the human origins of phenomena. For example, we tend to reify institutions such as colleges and universities, forgetting that these bureaucracies and other aspects of such institutional arrangements were, indeed, put together–that is, socially constructed—by real human beings.

relativism: Recognizes the diversity within social and conceptual worlds, that perspectives emerge out of distinct contexts. Cultural relativism, for example, refers to the fact that in a world of diverse cultures, there is a multiplicity of perspectives regarding what is right, good, true, etc. Often counterpointed with "absolutism" – that there is a specific, unalterable, truth.

representation: The process of forwarding an image or presentation of a particular phenomenon, giving it a public life, and perhaps even legitimacy and currency.

reproduction: Used here in the Marxist sense to refer to the complementary domain of production, i.e., the need for the worker to not only produce but that he or she must reproduce each day the capability to continue to work. This involves, therefore, the continued health and sustenance of the individual as well as his or her replacement, i.e., his or her children. Therefore, health and education are a fundamental part of capitalist reproduction.

resistance: In the sense used here needs to be counterpointed to **oppositional behaviour**. Resistance refers to action or presentation of ideas that emerge out of an analysis and comprehension of the complexities of social realities. Emergent opposition, therefore, debates and argues for greater social justice on the basis of clear understanding.

self-interest analysis: Distinct from **conspiracy theory**, self-interest analysis suggests that what may be perceived as conspiracy is, indeed, simply people acting on the basis of their own self-interest regarding social/political/economic life.

sign value: An increasingly important term as a result of the 'logo-ization' of our contemporary corporatist, consumer-based society. Within contemporary economic relationships the **exchange value** has obviously superseded **use value**. Sign value has begun to supersede both of these as we move to "branding," a term used to recognize that the marketplace is more competitive in terms of brand dominance than in terms of product dominance.

significant others: In George Herbert Mead's socialization theory, significant others are those people who are immediate to a child's experience, usually his or her parents or guardians. In Mead's presentation of socialization, "taking the role of the other" means, for the most part, taking the role of the significant other as a model.

social constructivism: Refers to the social scientific perspective which recognizes that little in social life or experience is pre-given (see **essentialism**) or established by divine right. Values, norms, mores, institutional structures, legal decisions, laws, etc. are, in fact, generated or constructed out of human/social energy, consciousness, and agency. For example, gendered expression in any society is culturally shared and agreed to, it is not natural.

social Darwinism: Perspective advocated by Herbert Spencer in his social application of Darwin's theory; in Spencer's terminology, "survival of the fittest" refers to the notion that certain individuals are fitter than others and that in times of social struggle, the fittest will survive. This perspective ignores the importance of **structural analysis**.

social democracy: In the political spectrum, social democracy may be seen as a more centrist or liberal perspective than that of **democratic socialism**, yet, still emerging out of the socialist, leftist political dynamic, it is reformist rather than revolutionary.

socialism: On the left of the political spectrum, socialism may be characterized by political demands that emerge out of social justice and equality, in general, advocating a fairer distribution of economic wealth and knowledge. Socialism often advocates for some or a good deal of public ownership of the means of production.

socialization theory: The social scientific theory that explains and explores the initiation and induction of the neophyte (new individual; infant/child) into the complexities of the socio-cultural world into which he or she is born. The process of socialization has been examined by several theorists from George Herbert Mead to Sigmund Freud to Erik Erikson. Its importance to the study of ideology seems crucial, particularly as we ask questions such as: To what ideologies have we been socialized?

sociology of knowledge: A complex sub-field of sociology most often associated with the work of Karl Marx and Karl Mannheim for its beginnings. Sociology of knowledge deals with the generation/production, formulation, legitimation, and dissemination of knowledge within society.

state: Often misunderstood as simply the government, the state encompasses much more than the government and includes institutions of education, the legal apparatus (including the courts, the police, and the prisons), the military, the overall bureaucracies of a particular nation, and the agencies of control and containment. For Weber (Gerth & Mills, 1990: 78; emphasis in original), the state had a "*monopoly of the legitimate use of physical force within a given territory.*"

state apparatus: A term originating with Louis Althusser, this recognizes that the arrangements, the organization, the bureaucracy, and the general infrastructure of the state is a mechanism or "apparatus" which can be effectively used both for and against any element under the state's jurisdiction.

structural theory: Refers to analysis that examines the significant structural dynamics in society's interactions, institutions, and relationships. It explores the organizational linkages and connections that make up the fabric — the warp and the weft —of the society. Structural analysis recognizes the patterns that evolve and generate the "way things are." In relationship to **conspiracy theory** and **self-interest theory**, structural analysis demands an account of phenomena based on structural relationships, rather than on relationships within groups or among individuals.

tabula rasa: The "blank slate" (originally explored by John Locke, the seventeenth-century British philosopher) onto which the society "writes" the codes of behaviour appropriate to the norms of that society. A particularly un-dialectical perspective regarding **socialization theory.**

taking the role of the other: George Herbert Mead's expression of the process whereby a child explores the events and happenings in the world and learns how to respond to these by seeing them through the eyes of their **significant other** or internalizing the response of their significant other.

The Sociological Imagination: The title of C. Wright Mills's classic work in sociology (1959). The phrase refers to the demand that students of social research need to situate themselves (their troubles and biographies) structurally and historically if they want to move to a new and more thorough comprehension of the workings of the social determinants of their lives.

theory of individuality: Recognition that the individual needs to be adequately situated within the collective, that the individual is in part defined by his or her community. In counterdistinction to the **ideology of individualism**, which assumes success and failure to be an egocentric moment, 'survival of the fittest', with the definition of what is "fit" individually defined.

three tricks: In Marx's study of ideology the three tricks explicate the process of mystification that envelopes people's everyday lives and moves them towards passive, uncritical acceptance of the world as it is.

transnational corporations (TNCs): Also known as multinational corporations (MNCs). Large corporate entities such as IBM, McDonald's, General Motors, Mitsubishi, Sony, Daimler-Benz, Wal-Mart, Nike, etc. that dominate world markets simply because of their size and economic wealth. For example, Wal-Mart's revenue is equivalent to the GDP of 161 countries (see *Beyond McWorld*, 1998). See **corporatization**.

tribalism: In postmodernist usage, a new form of ethnic **nationalism**, characterized by close identification with other members of the group for whom **identity politics** is crucial. Emergent is the group's power and "force" as a common front for political action.

use value: In the creation of necessary goods at the subsistence level, use value is need-related, and those objects produced are produced for individual or group use, but not for exchange in the market. See **exchange value** and **sign value**.

visible minorities: A contested term, referring to minority groups that are "**people of colour**," i.e., visibly identifiable and distinct from those who are "White."

References

Abercrombie, N., Hill, S., & Turner, B.S. (1988). *The Penguin dictionary of sociology*. London: Penguin.

Aidoo, A. A. (1972). The African woman today: An overview. *West Africa Journal*, 39, 1–7.

Althusser, L. (1969). *For Marx*. London: Allen Lane, The Penguin Press.

Alvord, K. (2000). *Divorce your car: Ending the love affair with the automobile*. Gabriola Island, BC: New Society Publishers.

Apple, M. (1979). *Ideology and curriculum*. London: Routledge & Keagan Paul.

Apple, M. (1982). *Education and power*. Boston: Routledge & Keagan Paul.

Aronowitz, S., & Giroux, H.A. (1985). *Education under siege: The conservative, liberal, and radical debate over schooling*. South Hadley, MA: Bergin & Garvey.

Bailey, G. (1986). Politicizing education. In W. Magnusson, Walker, R. B. J., Doyle, C., & De Marco, J. (Eds.). *After Bennett: A new politics for British Columbia* (296–312). Vancouver: New Star Books.

Bailey, G., & Gayle, N. (1993). *Sociology: An introduction from the classics to contemporary feminists*. Toronto: Oxford University Press.

Bannerji, H. (Ed.). (1993). *Returning the gaze: Essays on racism, feminism, and politics*. Toronto: Sister Vision Press.

Bannerji, H. (1995). *Thinking through: Essays on feminism, Marxism, and antiracism*. Toronto: Women's Press.

Barlow, M. (1991). *Parcel of rogues: How free trade is failing Canada*. Toronto: Key Porter Books.

Barlow, M. (1998). *The fight of my life*. Toronto: HarperCollins.

Barnett, R., & Müller, R. (1974). *Global reach: The power of the multinational corporations*. New York: Simon & Schuster.

Berger, J. (Narrator). (1974). *Ways of Seeing, Part 4* [Videorecording]. New York: Time Life Media, BBC.

Berger, P. (1967). *The sacred canopy: Elements of a sociological theory of religion*. New York: Anchor Books.

Berger, P., & Luckmann, T. (1967). *The social construction of reality: A treatise in the sociology of knowledge*. New York: Anchor Books.

Beyond McWorld: Challenging Corporate Rule [videorecording]. (1998). Council of Canadians & the Polaris Institute. Toronto: Just.In.Time Productions.

Bhabha, H. (1994). *The location of culture*. London & New York: Routledge.

Bhabha, H. (1999). Interview. In G. A. Olson & L. Worsham (Eds.), *Race, rhetoric, and the post colonial* (3–39). Albany, NY: State University of New York Press.

Blumer, H. (1969). *Symbolic interaction: Perspective and method*. Englewood Cliffs, NJ: Prentice-Hall.

Bolaria, B.S. (1995). *Social issues and contradictions in Canadian society* (2nd ed.). Toronto: Harcourt Brace & Company.

Bowers, C.A. (1987). *Elements of a post-liberal theory of education*. New York: Teachers College Press.

Bowles, S., & Gintis, H. (1976). *Schooling in capitalist America*. New York: Basic Books.

Boyd, S. (Ed.). (1997). *Challenging the public/private divide: Feminism, law, and public policy*. Toronto: University of Toronto Press.

Brand, D. (1993). A working paper on Black women in Toronto: Gender, race and class. In H. Bannerji (Ed.), *Returning the gaze: Essays on racism, feminism, and politics* (220–242). Toronto: Sister Vision Press.

Braverman, H. (1974). *Labor and monopoly capital: The degradation of work in the 20th century*. New York: Monthly Review Press.

Brym, R. (2001). *New society: Sociology for the 21st century*. Toronto: Harcourt Brace.

Burawoy, M. (1985). *The politics of production*. London: Verso.

Burke, E. (1790; 1969). *Reflections on the revolution in France* (C. O'Brien, Ed.). Harmondsworth: Penguin Books.

Burstyn, V. (1999). *The rites of men: Manhood, politics, and the culture of sport*. Toronto: University of Toronto Press.

Bush, G.W. (2001, September 20). Address to a Joint Session of Congress and the American People. (http://www.whitehouse.gov/news/releases/2001/09/print/20010920-8.html)

Carroll, W. K. (Ed.). (1997). *Organizing dissent: Contemporary social movements in theory and practice.* Toronto: Garamond Press.

Carroll, W.K. (2001). Personal communication.

Carty, L., & Brand, D. (1993). Visible minority women: A creation of the Canadian state. In H. Bannerji (Ed.), *Returning the gaze: Essays on racism, feminism, and politics* (169–81). Toronto: Sister Vision Press.

Cashmore, E., Banton, M., Jennings, J., Troyna, B., & Van Den Berghe, P. (1996). *Dictionary of race and ethnic relations* (4th ed.). London & New York: Routledge Books.

CBC. (1996, September 10). Town hall meeting. Transcript 961210, http://www.cbc.ca/national/transcripts/transcript

Chambers, I. (1986). *Popular culture: The metropolitan experience.* London and New York. Methuen.

Chomsky, N. (1989). *Necessary illusions: Thought control in democratic societies.* Toronto: CBC Enterprises.

Chomsky, N. (1999). *Profit over people: Neoliberalism and global order.* New York: Seven Stories Press.

Clarke, T. (1997). *The silent coup: Confronting the big business takeover of Canada.* Toronto: Canadian Centre for Policy Alternatives and James Lorimer & Company.

Cleaver, K.N. (1997). Racism, civil rights, and feminism. In A.K. Wing (Ed.). *Critical race feminism, A reader* (35–43). New York: New York University Press.

Cohen, L. (1999, May 1). *Globe and Mail,* C2

Cohen, R. (1997). The corporate takeover of news: Blunting the sword. In E. Barnouw, Aufderheide, P., Cohen, R., Thomas, F., Gitlin, T., Lieberman, D., Miller, M. C., Roberts, G., & Schatz, T. (Eds.). *Conglomerates and the media* (31–59). New York: The New Press.

Cooley, C.H. (1962). *Social organization: a study of the larger mind.* New York: Schocken Books.

Cooley, C.H. (1964). *Human nature and the social order.* New York: Schocken Books.

Davis, A. (1989). *Women, culture, and politics.* New York: Random House.

DeKeseredy, W.S., & Hinch, R. (1991). *Woman abuse: Sociological perspectives.* Toronto: Thompson Educational Publishing.

Dobbin, M. (1998). *The myth of the good corporate citizen: Democracy under the rule of big business.* Toronto: Stoddart.

Durkheim, E. (1912). *Elementary forms of religious life* (G. Simpson, Trans.). New York: The Free Press.

Eagleton, T. (1991). *Ideology: An introduction.* London: Verso.

Eisenstein, Z. (1981). *The radical future of liberal feminism.* New York: Longman.

Fairchild, H.P. (1977). *Dictionary of sociology.* Totowa, NJ: Littlefield, Adams & Company.

Farrell, S. (2001, November 28). Female general slams western feminists. *The Vancouver Sun,* Section A7.

Featherstone, M. (1995). *Undoing culture: Globalization, postmodernism and identity.* London: Sage Books.

Feagin, J.R. (1975). *Subordinating the poor: Welfare and American beliefs.* Englewood Cliffs, NJ: Prentice-Hall.

Fiske, J. (1989). *Understanding popular culture.* Boston: Unwin Hyman.

Foucault, M. (1972). *The archaeology of knowledge and the discourse of language.* New York: Harper & Row.

Foucault, M. (1979). *Discipline and punish: The birth of the prison.* New York: Vintage.

Foucault, M. (1980). *Power/knowledge: Selected interviews and other writings* (C. Gordon, Ed.). New York: Pantheon.

Freidan, B. (1963). *The feminine mystique.* New York: Dell Books.

Freire, P. (1970). *Cultural action for freedom.* Boston: Harvard Educational Review.

Freire, P. (1970). *Pedagogy of the oppressed.* New York: Seabury Press.

Freire, P. (1973). *Education: The practice of freedom.* London: Writers & Readers Publishing Cooperative.

Freire, P. (1998). *Pedagogy of freedom: Ethics, democracy, and civic courage.* New York: Rowman and Littlefield.

Friedman, M., & Friedman, R. (1981). *Free to choose.* New York: Avon Press.

Fyfe, S. (1998, January 3). *Globe and Mail,* D1.

Gablik, S. (1984). *Has modernism failed?* New York: Thames & Hudson.

Gayle, N. (1992). Black women's reality and feminism: An exploration of race and gender. In D. Currie & V. Raoul (Eds.), *Anatomy of gender: Women's struggle for the body* (232–42). Ottawa, ON: Carleton University Press.

Gayle, N. (1998). Representation and its impact: Making the case for third world women. In D. Currie, N. Gayle, & P. Gurstein (Eds.), *Learning to write: Women's studies in development* (37–48). Vancouver, BC: Collective Press.

Gerth H.H., & C. W. Mills. (Eds.). (1946). *From Max Weber: Essays in Sociology.* New York: Oxford University Press.

Giroux, H. (1981). *Ideology, culture, and the process of schooling.* Philadelphia, PA: Temple University Press.

Giroux, H. (1983). *Theory and resistance in education.* South Hadley, MA: Bergin & Garvey Publishers.

Giroux, H. (2000). *Stealing innocence: Youth, corporate power, and the politics of culture.* New York: St. Martin's Press.

Gitlin, Todd (1997). Introduction. In E. Barnouw, Aufderheide, P., Cohen, R., Thomas, F., Gitlin, T., Lieberman, D., Miller, M. C., Roberts, G. & Schatz, T. (eds.). *Conglomerates and the Media* (7–13). New York: The New Press.

Gledhill, C. (1997). Genre and gender: The case of the soap opera. In S. Hall (Ed.). *Representation: Cultural representations and signifying practices.* London: Sage Publications.

Glenday, D. & Duffy, A. (Eds.). (1994). *Canadian society: Understanding and surviving in the 1990s.* Toronto: McClelland & Stewart.

Gramsci, A. (1971). *Selections from the Prison Notebooks.* New York: International Publishers.

Griffin, S. (1982). The way of all ideology. *Signs: Journal of Women in Culture and Society* 7:3: 646–47.

Hale, S. (1995). *Controversies in sociology: A Canadian introduction* (2nd ed.). Mississauga, ON: Copp Clark.

Hall, S. (Ed.). (1997). *Representations: Cultural representations and signifying practices.* London: Sage Publications.

Hamilton, R. (1996). *Gendering the vertical mosaic: Feminist perspectives on Canadian society.* Toronto: Copp Clark.

Hardin, G. (1968). The tragedy of the commons. *Science,* 162, 1243–48.

Hebdige, D. (1979). *Sub-cultures: The meaning of style.* London: Routledge.

Henderson, H. (1991). *Paradigms in progress: Life beyond economics.* Indianapolis, IN: Knowledge Systems.

Henry, F., Tator, C., Matlis, W., & Rees, T. (1995/2000). *The colour of democracy: Racism in Canadian society* (2nd ed.). Toronto: Harcourt Brace.

Herman, E.S., & Chomsky, N. (1988). *Manufacturing consent: The political economy of the mass media.* New York: Pantheon Books.

Hiller, H. (1996). *Canadian society: A macro analysis.* Scarborough, ON: Prentice Hall Ltd.

Hill Collins, P. (1990). *Black feminist thought: Knowledge, consciousness, and the politics of empowerment.* Boston: Unwin Hyman Press.

Hoberman, J. (1997). *Darwin's athletes.* New York: Houghton Mifflin.

hooks, b. (1984). *Feminist theory: From margin to centre.* Boston, MA: South End Press.

hooks, b. (1988). *Talking back: Thinking feminist, thinking black.* Toronto: Between the Lines.

hooks, b. (1990). *Yearning: Race, gender, and cultural politics.* Toronto: Between the Lines.

hooks, b. (1992). *Black looks: Race and representation.* Toronto: Between the Lines.

hooks, b. (1994). *Teaching to transgress.* New York: Routledge.

hooks, b. (1997). *Cultural criticism and transformation.* [Videorecording]. Northhampton, MA: Media Education Foundation.

Husserl, E. (1967). *Phenomenology: The philosophy of Edmund Husserl* (J.J. Kockelmans, Ed.). New York: Doubleday.

Illich, I. (1974). *Energy and equity.* New York: Harper & Row.

James, C.E. (1999). *Seeing ourselves: Exploring race, ethnicity, and culture* (2nd ed.). Toronto: Thompson Educational Publishing.

Kilbourne, J. (Narrator.) (1974). *Killing us softly 3: Advertising's image of women* [Videorecording]. Northampton, MA: Cambridge Documentary Films.

King, D.K. (1997). Multiple jeopardy, multiple consciousness: the context of black feminist ideology. In D.T. Meyers (Ed.), *Feminist social thought: A reader* (219–42). New York: Routledge.

Klein, N. (2000). *No logo: Taking aim at the brand bullies.* Toronto: Knopf.

Knight, G. (2001). The mass media. In R. Brym (Ed.), *New society: Sociology for the 21st century* (89–116). Toronto: Harcourt.

Knutilla, M. (1992). *State theories: From liberalism to the challenge of feminism* (2nd ed.). Halifax, NS: Fernwood Publishers.

Kockelmans, J.J. (Ed.). (1967). *Phenomenology:The philosophy of Edmund Husserl.* New York: Doubleday.

Kozol, J. (1981). Foreword. In MacKie, R. (Ed.), *Literacy and revolution: The pedagogy of Paulo Freire.* New York: Continuum.

Lacey, N. (1993). Theory into Practice? Pornography and the Public/Private Dichotomy. *Journal of Law and Society* 20, 1: 93–113.

Lasn, K. (2000). *Culture jam.* New York: Quill.

Li, P. (1996). *The making of post-war Canada.* Toronto: Oxford University Press.

Lorde, A. (1983). The master's tools will never dismantle the master's house. In C. Moraga & G. Anzaldua (Eds.) *This bridge called my back: Writings of radical women of color* (98–101). New York: Kitchen Table, Women of Color Press.

Macedo, D. (1998). Foreword. In P. Freire, *Pedagogy of freedom: Ethics, democracy, and civic courage.* New York: Rowman & Littlefield.

MacKie, R. (Ed.). (1981). *Literacy and revolution: The pedagogy of Paulo Freire.* New York: Continuum.

Magnusson, W., & Sancton, A. (Eds.). (1983). *City politics in Canada.* Toronto: University of Toronto Press.

Mander, J. (1978). *Four arguments for the elimination of television.* New York: Quill.

Mannheim, K. (1936). *Ideology and utopia.* New York: Harcourt.

Marchak, P. (1988). *Ideological perspectives on Canada* (3rd ed.). Toronto: McGraw-Hill Ryerson.

Marcuse, H. (1964). *One-dimensional man: Studies in the ideology of advanced industrial society.* Boston, MA: Beacon Press.

Marx, K. (1967). *Capital: A critical analysis of capitalist production.* Vol 1 (F. Engels, Ed.). New York: International Publishers.

Marx, K. (1970). *Critique of Hegel's philosophy of right.* Cambridge, UK: Cambridge University Press.

Marx, K., & Engels, F. (1970). *The German ideology.* New York: International Publishers.

McLellan, D. (1973). *Karl Marx: His life and thought.* London: Macmillan Press.

McLellan, D. (1977). *Karl Marx: Selected writings.* New York: Oxford University Press.

Mead, G.H. (1934). *Mind, self, and society from the standpoint of a social behaviorist* (C.W. Morris, Ed.). Chicago, IL: University of Chicago Press.

Mernissi, F. (1994). *Dreams of trespass: Tales of a harem girlhood.* New York: Addison-Wesley.

Miliband, R. (1974). *The state in capitalist society.* London: Weidenfeld & Nicolson.

Mill, J.S. (1980). *The subjection of women.* (Sue Mansfield, Ed.). Arlington Heights, IL: AHM Publishing.

Miller, J. (1998). *Yesterday's news: Why Canada's daily newspapers are failing us.* Halifax: Fernwood Publishing.

Millet, K. (1971). *Sexual politics.* New York: Avon Press.

Mills, C.W. (1959). *The sociological imagination.* New York: Oxford University Press.

Mooers, C. (1998). Can we still resist? Globalization, citizenship rights, and class formation. *Socialist Studies Bulletin,* 53.

Monture, P.A. (1993). I know my name: A First Nations woman speaks. In G. Finn (Ed.), *Limited edition: Voices of feminism.* Halifax, NS: Fernwood Books.

Naiman, J. (1997). *How societies work: Class, power, and change in a Canadian context.* Concord, ON: Irwin Publishing.

Nietzsche, F. (1967). *The will to power.* (Walter Kaufmann, Ed.). New York: Vintage Books.

New York Times. (1999, March 21). Section 1, 18.

New Internationalist: The people, the ideas, the action in the fight for world development. (2001, November). Oxford: New Internationalist Publications Ltd.

O'Neale, S. (1986). Inhibiting midwives, usurping creators: The struggling emergence of black women in American fiction. In T. de Lauretis (Ed.), *Feminist studies/critical studies* (139–56). Bloomington, IN: Indiana University Press.

Oxford Universal Dictionary. (1933). London: Oxford University Press.

Palmer, H. (Ed.). (1975). *Immigration and the rise of multiculturalism.* Vancouver, BC: Copp Clark.

Panitch, L. (Ed.). (1977). *The Canadian state: Political economy and political power.* Toronto: University of Toronto Press.

Parenti, M. (1993). *Inventing reality: The politics of news* (2nd ed.). New York: St. Martin's Press.

Postman, N. (1979). *Teaching as a conserving activity.* New York: Delacorte Press.

Postman, N. (1982). *The disappearance of childhood*. New York: Dell Publishing.

Postman, N., & Powers, S. (1992). *How to watch TV news*. New York: Penguin.

Poulantzas, N. (1973). *Political power and social classes*. London: NLB.

Poulantzas, N. (1975). *Classes in contemporary capitalism*. London: NLB.

Pupo, N. (1994). Dissecting the role of the state. In D. Glenday & A. Duffy (Eds.), *Canadian society: Understanding and surviving in the 1990s*. Toronto: McClelland & Stewart.

Ramazanoglu, C. (1989). *Feminism and the contradictions of oppression*. London: Routledge.

Razack, S. (Ed.). (2002). *Race, space, and the law: Unmapping a white settler society*. Toronto: Between the Lines.

Rebick, J. (2000). *Imagine democracy*. Toronto: Stoddart.

Resnick, P. (2000). *The politics of resentment: British Columbia regionalism and Canadian unity*. Vancouver, BC: University of British Columbia Press.

Richer, S. & Weir, L. (1995). *Beyond political correctness: Toward the inclusive university*. Toronto: University of Toronto Press.

Rifkin, J. (1995). *The end of work: The decline of the global labor force and the dawn of the post-market era*. New York: G.P. Putnam & Sons.

Ritzer, G. (1993). *The McDonaldization of society*. Newbury Park, CA: Pine Forge Press.

Rushkoff, D. (1996). *Media virus: Hidden agendas in popular culture*. New York: Balentine Books.

Said, E. (1979). *Orientalism*. New York: Vintage Books.

Said, E. (1981). *Covering Islam*. New York: Pantheon Books.

Said, E. (1994). *The pen and the sword : Conversations with David Barsamian*. Toronto: Between the Lines.

Saint-Simon, H. (1952). *Selected writings* (F.M.H. Markham, Ed.). London: Basil Blackwell.

Sarup, M. (1996). *Identity, culture, and the postmodern world*. Edinburgh: Edinburgh University Press.

Satzewich, V. (Ed.). (1998). *Racism and social inequality in Canada*. Toronto: Thompson Educational Publishing.

Saul, J.R. (1993). *Voltaire's bastards: The dictatorship of reason in the west*. Toronto: Penguin Books.

Saul, J.R. (1994). *The doubter's companion: A dictionary of aggressive common sense.* Toronto: Penguin Books.

Saul, J.R. (1995). *The unconscious civilization.* Concord, ON: Anansi.

Saul, J.R. (1997a). *Reflections of a Siamese twin: Canada at the end of the twentieth century.* Toronto: Penguin Books.

Saul, J.R. (1997b). The good citizen. *Canadian Forum,* December.

Schiller, H. (1973). *The mind managers.* Boston, MA: Beacon Press.

Schumacher, E. F. (1973). *Small is beautiful: Economics as if people mattered.* New York: Harper & Row.

Scruton, R. (1982). *A dictionary of political thought.* London: Macmillan.

Seabrook, J. (2002). *The no-nonsense guide to class, caste and hierarchies.* New York: W.W. Norton.

Shapiro, J.S. (1958). *Liberalism: Its meaning and history.* Toronto: D. Van Nostram Company.

Shiva, V. (1997). *Biopiracy: The plunder of nature and knowledge.* Toronto: Between the Lines.

Smith, D. (1977). *Feminism and Marxism: A place to begin, A way to go.* Vancouver, BC: New Star Books.

Smith, D. (1987). *The everyday world as problematic: A feminist sociology.* Toronto: University of Toronto Press.

Smith, D. (1990). *The conceptual practices of power: A feminist sociology of knowledge.* Toronto: University of Toronto Press.

Spence, C.M. (1999). *The skin I'm in: Racism, sports, and education.* Halifax, NS: Fernwood Publishing.

Stoppard, J. (1992). A suitable case for treatment? Premenstrual syndrome and the medicalization of women's bodies. In D. Currie & V. Raoul (Eds.,), *Anatomy of gender: Women's struggle for the body.* Ottawa, ON: Carleton University Press.

Strauss, A. (Ed.). (1964). *The social psychology of George Herbert Mead.* Chicago, IL: University of Chicago Press.

Teeple, G. (1995). *Globalization and the decline of social reform.* Toronto: Garamond Press.

Teeple, G. (2000). *Globalization and the decline of social reform: Into the twenty-first century* (2nd ed.). Aurora, ON: Garamond Press.

Tepperman, L. & Blaine, J. (1999). *Think twice: Sociology looks at current social issues.* Upper Saddle River, NJ: Prentice-Hall.

Theodorson, G.A., & Theodorson, A.G. (1969). *A modern dictionary of sociology.* New York: Barnes & Noble Books.

Todd, D. (1999, June 26). The truth about lying: Often it pays off or is left unpunished. *Vancouver Sun,* 7–8.

Totten, M. (2000). *Guys, Gangs, and Girlfriend Abuse.* Peterborough, ON: Broadview Press.

Twitchell, J.B. (1996). But first, a word from our sponsor: Advertising and the carnivalization of culture. In K. Washburn & J. Thornton (Eds.), *Dumbing down: Essays on the strip-mining of American culture* (197–208). New York: W.W. Norton.

von Hayek, F. (1955). *The counter-revolution of science: Studies on the abuse of reason.* London: The Free Press.

West, C. (1994). *Race matters.* New York: Vintage.

West, C. (1993). The new cultural politics of difference. In S. During (Ed.), *The cultural studies reader* (203–17). London: Routledge.

Williams, R. (1974). *Television: Technology and cultural forms.* Glasgow: Fontana/Collins.

Williams, R. (1976). *Keywords: A vocabulary of culture and society.* Glasgow: Fontana Books.

Willis, P. (1981). *Learning to labor: How working class kids get working class jobs.* New York: Columbia University Press.

Wilson, Alexander. (1991). *The culture of nature: North American landscape from Dysney to the Exxon Valdez.* Toronto: Between the Lines.

Wilson, J.R. (1995). *The myth of political correctness: The conservative attack on higher education.* Durham, NC: Duke University Press.

Woodcock, G. (1988). *A Social History of Canada.* Toronto: Penguin Books.

Index